Church
Financial
Management

Church Financial Management

A Practical Guide for Today's Church Leaders

Geoffrey V. Guns

PROVIDENCE HOUSE PUBLISHERS
Franklin, Tennessee

Copyright 1997 by Geoffrey V. Guns

Printed in the United States of America

01   5   4   3

Library of Congress Catalog Card Number: 97-76458

ISBN: 1–57736–061–3

Cover by Gary Bozeman

Third Printing 2001

PROVIDENCE HOUSE PUBLISHERS
238 Seaboard Lane • Franklin, Tennessee 37067
800-321-5692

To
Rosetta, Kimberly, and Nicole

Your patience with me is a blessing!

Contents

Preface and Acknowledgments   ix

Introduction   xi

   1. Understanding Financial Management   3

   2. Biblical Foundations for Effective Financial Management   11

   3. The Duties of Church Leaders   20

   4. The Functions of Money Management   34

   5. Developing and Administering the Church Budget   44

   6. Paying the Pastor and the Church Staff   62

   7. Church Construction: A Pastor's Dream or Nightmare   86

Epilogue   95

Bibliography   96

Preface and Acknowledgments

The one question that a lot of people will ask is "Why would anyone want to go to the trouble to write another book about church administration?" Hopefully, you will read it and discover why. This book is written from the experiential perspective of a pastor. I have tried to incorporate nearly eighteen years of experience in the pastoral ministry in this effort. The book is filled with a number of practical ideas and suggestions that may be helpful to all pastors, young and old, black and white.

This book is written with laypeople in mind as well. I have intentionally avoided a lot of technical language. The whole purpose of the book is to assist the laity in coming to grips with the complexities of church financial management. Granted there are some large churches and mega churches that can hire a full-time staff person to take care of this ministry. However, the majority of us are pastors and members of churches where the work is done by volunteers and underpaid staff persons. Hopefully, my work will encourage them by providing suggestions for working more effectively.

I want to take this opportunity to thank God for allowing me the privilege to preach and teach His Word. I am, indeed, indebted to my many friends and colleagues who have afforded me opportunities to share many of these ideas in workshops and seminars. I am equally grateful to the many church leaders across the country who have been in conferences with me and helped shape and sharpen my thinking.

I am especially indebted to Second Calvary Church which has allowed me to be their pastor for the past thirteen years. They have followed me and given me a great deal of support in this effort. A lot of the ideas have been developed and incorporated at Second Calvary, and have been found to work effectively.

There are several members of the church who took time to read the manuscript and offered their suggestions. I am grateful to Stephanie Jackson, and Donna Williams for their patience and encouragement. Rosetta, my wife, has been a great source of inspiration and help. I want to thank my friend Dr. Mark Croston for sharing some of his ideas with me, and also Dr. Robert G. Murray who took the time to read the manuscript. I am grateful to Dr. John Kinney of the school of theology at Virginia Union University for reading the manuscript. I want to thank you the reader for taking the time to read this book. May God bless you!

Introduction

One of the biggest challenges facing the church today is the establishment and implementation of sound financial management and administrative procedures. The world in which we live, particularly the financial world, has changed dramatically over the past twenty years. Increasingly, churches have to be more efficient and effective in the management of all of their resources. Today, church leaders must deal with intense pressure from members, who want and deserve strict accountability of the money they give for the Lord's work. Further, the federal government and many state governments require that churches meet certain standards of accountability and fiscal responsibility.

Tax laws and filing requirements are increasingly a part of the everyday conduct of church business affairs. The changes in the tax laws have left many churches in violation of basic filing requirements. As church staffs increase and full-time ministry becomes a way of life for many church workers, the church must deal with employee matters, salary packages, benefit plans, and a host of employer/employee issues.

The complexity of these and many other issues means that there is a real need for a different and new kind of church leader and administrator. When I was a seminary student, I recall taking only one course in church administration and virtually nothing in the area of leadership. Much of my seminary education, like that of many other seminary students, was in the area of biblical exegesis, church history, homiletics, practical theology, Old and New Testament and other biblical courses. Consequently, many seminary graduates are ill-prepared for the stark realities of leading and managing in today's church environment. Just as many pastors are ill-equipped, so is the army of volunteer church leaders who work full-time jobs, come to the church at the end of their work day and feel that they have a grip on what ought to be done.

Fortunately, for me, I earned a degree in business administration which gave me many of the tools needed to understand the fundamentals of sound financial management. Additionally, I spent six years in the U.S. Army as a commissioned officer which enabled me to learn the fundamentals of leadership. Lastly, I was a battalion personnel administrator, commonly referred to as the S-1, which enabled me to see the importance of sound personnel administration. I do not claim to be an expert in this field, only a practitioner of basic financial management.

This guide is an attempt to bridge the gap between theory and reality. It is not the ultimate and concluding word on church financial management. However, it is an attempt to provide a framework for the local pastor and the church's leaders to begin the process of better equipping themselves for more effective ministry and management of the resources entrusted in our care. The guidelines and suggestions made in this guide can be used by both the young inexperienced pastor and the seasoned veteran who needs a tool to train and update the skills of his leaders.

There are seven chapters in the guide. In Chapter One, I define financial management and set forth the benefits of sound financial management. Also, I list ten hindrances to effective financial management and the solution to the problems.

Chapter Two examines the biblical teachings regarding sound financial management. It is an attempt to lay out a biblical foundation for how we are to use the Lord's money. In Chapter Three, a list of the duties and responsibilities of the key leaders involved in financial management are set forth. The information contained in this chapter is crucial for determining the lines of responsibility and authority of financial leaders. In Chapter Four a brief description of the functions of effective money management are laid out. Chapter Five details some of the requirements and procedures that can be followed in developing and adopting an annual church budget. Chapter Six discusses the biblical mandate for the church to be just and fair with how it compensates its pastor and staff. It is not a complete guide to this very important area; it is however a primer for more intense examination. In Chapter Seven I discuss church construction projects and how they go from being every pastor's dream to becoming a nightmare.

God has called us to go into all the world and preach and teach the gospel of salvation to a lost and sinful world. However, there are costs associated with carrying the gospel to a broken and fallen humanity. And wherever there is money, there must be accountability. I pray that this guide will help put you on the road to greater confidence in developing programs of responsible financial management.

"But let all things be done properly and in an orderly manner."
1 Corinthians 14:40

Church
Financial
Management

Chapter One

Understanding
Financial Management

"Taking precaution that no
one should discredit us in our
administration. . . ."
— *2 Corinthians 8:20*

Sound and efficient financial management is one of the least practiced disciplines in the local church. One reason is due to our lack of training in the area. It is absolutely essential that church leaders know how to raise and spend the money that is collected for the work of the ministry. Financial management is nothing but a formal way of talking about our financial stewardship. In Christian stewardship, we are concerned with the wise and proper use of all of God's gifts, i.e. spiritual gifts, natural talents, and time. We are also concerned with how the church uses what God has entrusted to it for the work of the ministry.

One of the biggest challenges that the apostle Paul had to contend with were questions regarding his personal integrity in handling the offering that was being collected for the poor saints in Jerusalem. This was of obvious concern to the Corinthians, who raised the issue. In his second letter to the church at Corinth, he assured them of his personal honesty. Paul went to great lengths to squelch any questions regarding his improper handling of the offering. He sent Titus and a highly respected brother (whose name we do not know) to prepare the Corinthians for his arrival to receive the offering. In 2 Corinthians 8:16–22, Paul detailed how he would guard his reputation concerning the offering that was being collected for the saints in Jerusalem.

"But thanks be to God, who puts the same earnestness on your behalf in the heart of Titus. For he not only accepted our appeal, but being himself very earnest, he has gone to you of his own accord. And we have sent along with him the brother whose fame in the things of the gospel has spread through all the churches; and not only this, but he has also been appointed by the churches to travel with us in this gracious work, which is being administered by us for the glory of the Lord Himself, and to show our readiness, taking precaution that no one should discredit us in our administration of this generous gift; for we have regard for what is honorable, not only in the sight of the Lord, but also in the sight of men. And we have sent with them our brother, whom we have often tested and found diligent in many things, but now even more diligent, because of his great confidence in you." (2 Cor. 8:16–22)

Clearly, Paul demonstrated glowing financial managerial ability. He did not give the Corinthians any reason to raise further questions about his integrity by virtue of the manner in which he handled the offering. The people that he sent ahead of himself were men with impeccable personal credentials. They were highly regarded and in fact had been selected by the churches to undertake this project. There is no doubt that they were selected because they had a record of being good stewards of the money collected for the Lord's work.

Whenever the church chooses leaders to handle the financial resources of the church, they should be persons whose character and integrity are impeccable and of the highest standard.

NOT-FOR-PROFIT VERSUS FOR-PROFIT

Is the church a business? Or is the church a religious and spiritual enterprise whose sole mission is to preach and teach the gospel? I would answer that the church is both. It is indeed a business whose sole purpose is the proclamation of the gospel of salvation. Yet, it must be remembered that the church is not a traditional for-profit business. However, those who are charged with managing the financial resources of the church are responsible to ensure that the principles of sound business and financial management are utilized.[1]

As Bramer pointed out, "Every dollar saved by more efficient management of the church plant, for example, means another dollar freed for Christian education material."[2] Inefficient plant management is one of the leading causes of waste in the church, which in turn, reduces the amount of money available for ministry and missions.

There is a vast difference between a for-profit corporation or business and a not-for-profit corporation. Oftentimes, persons who are elected to serve as church trustees and have managerial positions in everyday life want to bring the same "downsizing mentality" to the church's operation that is going on in the business world. Therefore, a great deal of time is spent looking at how to cut the budget as opposed to increasing revenues for greater Christian service. Christ has commissioned the church to grow, not to shrink (see Matt. 28:19–20; Acts 1:5–8; 2:47).

My wife and I invest in the U.S. stock market. One of the things we look for in a company that we are considering for investment is revenue growth. How fast is the company growing its profits and is it in a business where it has a competitive advantage? Does the particular company that we intend to invest in have a decided advantage in the quality of its product or service? Businesses exist purely for the sake of making a profit and increasing value for its shareholders. In fact, management is evaluated on its ability to increase the value of the individual shares of company stock. Companies that are growing very rapidly will reinvest their profits back into the business to increase their competitive advantage, thereby increasing market share and profits. Companies that are able to grow and adjust to changing market environments will always be very profitable.

The church, para-church organization or any not-for-profit corporation has an entirely different mission than a for-profit business. The church is in the business of altering lives. Peter Drucker stated that, "The non-profit organization exists to bring about a change in individuals and in society."[3] The sole purpose of the church is to present the gospel of salvation, which is able to radically change the lives of men and women (see 1 Cor. 5:17). The church is not in the business of accumulating assets purely for the sake of accumulating them. When the church becomes concerned about what it has amassed, it becomes like the man Jesus called a fool in the parable of the rich fool in Luke 12:13–21. "Any retention of income should be for the sole purpose of maintaining or increasing service in the near future."[4] Church leaders must remember that the church does not exist to make a profit but to make a difference in the lives of people.

WHAT IS FINANCIAL MANAGEMENT?

Money is a major problem in many churches. The problem exists on two fronts. The first is concerned with how funds are raised. The second is concerned with how it is spent and who makes the determination regarding spending priorities. Fund raising and spending are both constituent elements of financial management. One cannot exist without the other. I define financial management as those procedures that facilitate the proper planning, organizing, controlling and directing of the money collected by the church. Further, it takes into account the need to gain the maximum return for each dollar raised and spent. Consider Peter R. Peacock's definition of financial management.[5]

> Financial management is determining what financial needs must be met in the current year, identifying sources of funds to meet those needs, establishing a procedure to raise the money, making adjustments in spending and/or fund-raising if anticipated income does not match financial needs, and maintaining control over income and expenditures.

Inefficient financial management leads to waste management. Churches that do not take seriously the need for sound financial management ultimately spend more of the Lord's money needlessly. Strong churches are well-managed and insist on strict accountability in the use of their resources. A lot of money is wasted in churches simply through inefficient and poor managerial habits. Unfortunately, many churches are notoriously guilty of wasting a lot of their financial resources through inefficient plant and personnel management.

Key Words in Financial Management

The field of financial management has its own language. We may not be entirely familiar with all of the words used in financial management. I want to list some of the common words that are used and offer a brief definition. This list is by far very short compared to the whole field of words used in the field of financial management.

Management. Management is the art and science of planning for, organizing and directing the personnel and resources of an organization toward the successful accomplishment of a specific task or mission. Management is doing things the right way so as to ensure success.

Controlling. Controlling refers to the processes used to ensure that the proper steps and procedures are followed in the collection, counting, depositing, recording, and spending of the church's money. Controlling provides the necessary safeguards to ensure that church funds are protected from theft or waste. Controlling ensures that everything is done in accordance with the church's annual spending plan. Churches without adequate financial controls are generally out of control. When spending is out of control, the church is courting financial disaster.

Fiduciary Responsibility. Fiduciary responsibility refers to the committed trust that is placed with the persons charged with properly managing the church's resources. In the church, the pastor, trustees, treasurer, and financial secretary (bookkeeper) all bear responsibility for how the financial resources of the church are handled. Unless financial leaders are held accountable for how they handle the church's money, the possibility for waste and abuse exists.

Financial Planning. Financial planning refers to the process of determining the short and long term financial goals of the church through the establishment of intentional spending and investing priorities. In this competitive financial environment all churches need to develop adequate financial plans. Churches without short and long-term financial plans will continue to struggle financially. Planning does not eliminate uncertainty in the political, social and economic environment; it helps the church to adjust more readily to changes. Planning can help the church to adapt to changes in the local economy or demographic changes that can hit the church.

The Benefits of Financial Management

Peter Peacock has identified three benefits of sound financial management.[6] First, good financial management enables the church to take a more reasoned approach in the conduct of its affairs. It permits that church to give attention to and allocate resources to those activities and events that demand more time and money.

Second, good financial management enables the church to make adjustments to changing local economic conditions. A local church can be negatively impacted in several ways. During the winter of 1996 the weather produced several major snow storms. In Virginia Beach where I live, we experienced two consecutive months, January and February, in which snow and ice storms occurred during the month. Much of the business news centered around how much money had been lost by corporations, yet thousands of churches were closed up and down the East Coast. This meant that tens of millions of dollars did not reach church collection plates. The storms hit during the days leading up to the first Sunday of the month, which is the number one collection Sunday of the month for every church in the country. Churches without cash reserves felt the pinch for much of the year. Generally, when churches are closed due to weather, chances are many of those funds are permanently lost. Granted most people will honor their pledge to the church, and will not present a significant financial concern to the church.

Third, good financial management contributes to the annual stewardship drive. The wise and prudent use of church funds focuses attention on the ministries and mission programs of the church.

Fourth, good financial management builds confidence in the church's leadership who are handling church funds. When members feel that what they give is being properly used they will have no problems giving to support the work of the church's ministry.

Fifth, good financial management promotes church growth. There is nothing that contributes to membership departures like the perception that money is being mishandled or poorly managed. Likewise the public perception that a church's leadership is honest in handling money can contribute to church growth. This extends to the timely issuance of periodic financial reports and the perception that the leaders have nothing to hide. Sometimes pastors will not stress the importance of timely and accurate financial reports being published. I cannot stress this enough; financial reports are essential to members feeling that the leadership has integrity.

Hindrances to Effective Financial Management
In order for effective and efficient financial management to take place, there are a number of hindrances that must be overcome. In

some churches, all may be present and in others only a few may be present. This list consists of ten objections that I have heard over the years as a pastor and as a workshop and conference leader in the area of stewardship and leadership training. The list will require no explanation; the objections are their own best commentary.

1. Lack of pastoral leadership and direction.
2. Lack of training on the part of financial leaders.
3. Poorly conceived and executed spending plans.
4. Resistance to change and progress.
5. Power struggles over control of the church's money.
6. Absence of effective internal controls.
7. Lack of short-and long-term financial planning.
8. Failure to understand the current economic climate and its impact upon the church's ministry.
9. Misplaced values and priorities—money ahead of ministries and missions.
10. Unclear lines of authority and responsibility.

The Single Solution

There is only one solution for each of the hindrances listed above and that is leadership training that concentrates on the principles of contemporary church financial management. Church leaders should be trained to understand the biblical mission and mandate of the church. Further they should know and understand their local church's mission and the strategies for achieving it. How the church uses its financial resources is directly related to an understanding of its mission. When it comes to financial management, the church is its own worst enemy. We will put people in key positions of financial responsibility without regard for qualifications or training. If there is going to be a change in the problems that we have with financial management in churches, it has to begin with boldness on the part of the pastor. He or she has to lead in this regard by becoming educated in basic business management, accounting, bookkeeping, financial reporting, Internal Revenue Service reporting requirements, etc. Unless the leader is knowledgeable, he or she cannot even begin to help the church's leaders.

My single solution does not leave out the spiritual dimensions of prayer and study of God's Word to discover biblical truths regarding proper stewardship of the Lord's money. In fact, the Word of God is the foundation of our understanding regarding the proper exercise of our fiduciary responsibilities (see Matt. 25: 14–30; Luke 16:1ff; 1 Cor. 4:2). The Word of God is full of examples of godly men who were charged with stewardship responsibility. In the book of Genesis we read how Joseph was charged with the stewardship of his master's property (see Gen. 39:1–6). Joseph was such a good steward that his master did not even concern himself with his property. He knew that Joseph would do the right things (vs. 6). God expects us to do the right things with the resources that have been entrusted to our care.

NOTES

1. John C. Bramer Jr., *Efficient Church Business Management* (Philadelphia: Westminster Press, 1960), pp. 11–12.

2. Ibid., p. 12.

3. Peter F. Drucker, *Managing The Non-Profit Organization* (New York: HarperCollins Publishers, 1990), p. 3.

4. Bramer, op. cit., p. 13.

5. Peter R. Peacock, "Annual Financial Management," in *Managing Today's Church*, ed. Robert N. White, (Valley Forge: Judson Press, 1981), p. 52.

6. Ibid. pp. 52–53.

Chapter Two

Biblical Foundations for Effective Financial Management

"Moreover, it is required of stewards that one be found trustworthy."

—*1 Corinthians 4:2*

Theology is by definition the study of the doctrine of God. It is the examination and interpretation of the meaning of the Scriptures and their impact upon the lives of believers. A biblical theology of church financial management begins with a basic understanding of Christian stewardship. Church leaders, under the leadership of the pastor, are responsible for management of the church's resources.

The leadership of the local church bears a major stewardship responsibility for the management of their personal lives and personal resources (see 1 Tim. 3:3–13, esp. verse 5; Acts 6:3; 20:28). Stewardship begins at home. The church's leaders must be taught the dynamic principles of church financial management. Just as the saints must be equipped for the work of the ministry, so must leaders be equipped to manage the church's financial resources (see Eph. 4:11–12).

Therefore, our understanding of church financial management grows out of the Bible's teachings on Christian stewardship. Paul wrote to the Corinthians that faithfulness is an essential trait for the steward to possess. In fact it was not an option. In 1 Corinthians 4:2 he wrote, "Now it is required that those who have been given a trust prove faithful" (NIV).

Biblical stewardship takes into account three important aspects of Christian Stewardship. First, the members of a local church's understanding of biblical stewardship will never be any greater than that of

11

its leadership. If the leadership of the church has a narrow steward-ship focus, the members will more than likely have the same narrow focus.

Second, the understanding of the members is shaped by what they have been taught by the pastor and what they believe about God and His purposes for their individual and corporate lives. The pastor does a major disservice to the kingdom of God and himself when he or she fails at the point of teaching. The success of Jesus' ministry was the result of his teaching (see Matt. 4:23–25; 5:2).

Third, the stewardship practices of the individual members will never exceed that of the expectations of the church's leadership. If there are no expectations of growth in every area of the members' spiritual development, then the members will fall to those levels of stewardship mediocrity.

The task of managing the church's financial resources should be carried on by a financial management team. It is not the responsibility of a single person, or two or three people for that matter. The pastor should take the central role in managing the financial affairs of the church. In too many churches the role or place of the pastor has been reduced to that of just preacher/teacher. The administrative functions have been stripped from him and given to others who may have no idea of the Lord's vision for His church. We must begin to educate the members of the local church as to the biblical portrait of the pastor as the church's key spiritual leader. The pastor's office must be restored to a position of spiritual primacy in the local church.

PASTOR/OVERSEER

In many churches, the office of pastor has fallen to new lows of disrespect and outright contempt by some members. Unfortunately, there are some people who have been mistakenly led to believe that deacons, trustees and in some cases church finance committees, "run the church." I am not quite sure as to what that means other than it is a neat way of saying we must keep the preacher in check. This extremely false and biblically unsound practice is detrimental to the spiritual and financial health of the local church. We cannot develop a practical approach to financial management without first recognizing the biblical priority attached to the office of the pastor.

In some cases men and women are getting caught up on the proper title to be used for the pastor's office. Is he or she to be called a reverend, bishop, presbyter, elder, preacher, or what? I want to suggest that while these are certainly important, they are mere side issues. The larger issue has to do with how we understand the office and what the Bible teaches about the office and role of the pastor. The Bible is our sole source of information for instruction and direction regarding the role and place of the office of pastor.

For the sake of our interests, I want to examine biblical teachings that address the primacy of the pastor/overseer. The reader is encouraged to continue his or her quest for understanding since this will not be an exhaustive and conclusive study. The office of pastor/overseer is biblical and deserves the highest respect and regard.

WHAT IS A PASTOR?

When I first accepted my call to the ministry, all I could think about was being a pastor. I had watched my father pastor a congregation for years and figured that I had a pretty good idea of what was involved. Even during my years in seminary, the one thing that I wanted to do was to pastor a congregation. I knew that I had the skills and the personality to be a good pastor. Unfortunately, nothing I had done up to the time I was called to my first church prepared me for what I was about to enter. Over the years I have had to study and learn what the Bible says about what it means to be a pastor. Further, I have had to teach the church the biblical principles regarding the pastor's office and calling.

Many men and women are frustrated in their pastoral settings because they are dealing with congregations who have little or no idea of who the pastor is, what he is called to do, and his place of primacy within the local congregation. There may be many leaders within the local church, but there can only be one pastor. When you have too many leaders seeking to be the pastor, the church becomes confused, misdirected and thrown into chaos.

In 3 John 9 there is mention of a church leader by the name of Diotrephes who became a disruptive and divisive presence in his church. He was a man who would not submit to the authority of the apostle John or anyone else for that matter. The apostle had evidently written a letter to the church that Diotrephes either intercepted or would not allow to be read. In 3 John 9–10 we read, "I wrote to the church, but Diotrephes, who loves to be first, will have nothing to do with us. So if I come, I will call attention to what he is doing, gossiping maliciously about us. Not satisfied with that, he refuses to welcome the brothers. He also stops those who want to do so and put them out of the church" (NIV). John R. W. Stott remarked that Diotrephes claimed an authority of his own and that he was not going to be dictated by the apostle John.[1] There are people today in churches who have this same attitude. They refuse to follow the leadership of the pastor.

The Biblical Definition

According to *Vine's Expository Dictionary of New Testament Words,* the word pastor is from the Greek word, *poimena* and it means the following:

> a shepherd, one who tends herds or flocks (not merely one who feeds them), is used metaphorically of Christian "pastors," Eph. 4:11. Pastors guide as well as feed the flock; cp. Acts 20:28, which, with ver. 17, indicates that this was the service committed to elders (overseers or bishops); so also in 1 Pet. 5:1–2, "tend the flock . . . exercising the oversight," R.V.; this involves tender care and vigilant superintendence.[2]

In the New Testament there are references to what some believe to be three distinct leadership offices, i.e. bishop, elder, and pastor. Space nor time will permit an exhaustive study of the words and their usage in the New Testament. Several biblical scholars have done excellent work on the matter and their work is more than sufficient.[3]

Indeed, John MacArthur, an excellent biblical scholar has clearly pointed out that the words bishop, pastor, and elder all point to the same person.[4]

> Bishops and pastors are not distinct from elders; the terms are simply different ways of identifying the same people. The Greek

word for *bishop* is *episkospos,* from which the Episcopalian Church gets its name. The Greek word for *pastor* is *poimen.*

The textual evidence indicates that all three terms refer to the same office. The qualifications for a bishop, listed in 1 Timothy 3:1–7, and those for an elder, in Titus 1:6–9, are unmistakably parallel. In fact, in Titus, Paul uses both terms to refer to the same man (1:5, 7).

First Peter 5:1–2 brings all three terms together: "Therefore, I exhort the elders [*presbuteros*] among you, as your fellow-elder and witness of the suffers of Christ, and a partaker also of the glory that is to be revealed, shepherd [*poimaino*] the flock of God among you, exercising oversight [*episkopeo*] not under compulsion, but voluntarily, according to the will of God."[5]

It is important that we understand that the title we use for the office of the pastor is secondary to the more weighty matter of what his or her place is within the church. Some would say that the pastor is merely the spiritual leader of the church. As James H. Harris has pointed out:

The minister is more than the "spiritual leader" in the church. He or she is the leader, spiritual and administrative. There is no theological basis for dichotomizing the work of the ministry into spiritual and secular realms.[6]

What is a pastor? The pastor is someone who has been called by God to lead His people in the accomplishment of His will and purposes. As God's called, anointed, and appointed leader for His people, the pastor has the oversight of the entire church. The people of God are under biblical authority to follow and submit to the leadership of their pastor. This is clearly taught in the New Testament. In Hebrews 13:17 of the New American Standard Version of the Bible we read, "Obey your leaders, and submit to them; for they keep watch over your souls, as those who will give an account. Let them do this with joy and not with grief, for this would be unprofitable for you."

In Acts 20:28 the apostle Paul told the elders of Ephesus at Miletus, "Be on guard for yourselves and for all the flock, among which the Holy Spirit has made you overseers, to shepherd the church of God which He purchased with His own blood" (NASV).

Clearly, the Bible teaches that God has given the pastor the central role of leadership. He exercises that responsibility effectively when the members of the local church give assent to the Bible's teachings. As James Harris has indicated, the pastor is called to lead God's people, not follow boards or the people.[7]

BIBLICAL TENETS OF FINANCIAL MANAGEMENT

The basic tenets of financial management are grounded in Scripture. The Bible must be the determining factor and guide for all we do and believe. "All Scripture is inspired by God and profitable for teaching, for reproof, for correction, for training in righteousness; that the man of God may be adequate, equipped for every good work" (2 Timothy 3:16–17, NASV).

Tenets are beliefs that we hold to be truth. They are the standard by which the Christian faith is practiced. The tenets that follow are the result of my own understanding of the Bible's teachings on this vital subject. I have listed six tenets that I believe are central for the development of a mature understanding of church financial management.

Tenet Number One

Leaders are required to wisely and faithfully manage resources entrusted to their care.

The biblical basis:

> In this case, moreover, it is required of stewards that one be found trustworthy. (1 Cor. 4:2)

> We must all appear before the judgment seat of Christ, that each one may be recompensed for his deeds in the body, according to what he has done, whether good or bad. (2 Cor. 5:10)

Tenet Number Two
    Leaders should demonstrate sound, personal stewardship before being charged to manage church financial resources.

The biblical basis:

> He must be one who manages his own household well, keeping his children under control with all dignity (but if a man does not know how to manage his own household, how will he take care of the church of God?). (1 Tim. 3:4–5)

Tenet Number Three
    Leaders are required to give more of themselves and their personal resources as an example for others to follow.

The biblical basis:

> Then King David said to the entire assembly, "My son Solomon, whom alone God has chosen, is still young and inexperienced and the work is great; for the temple is not for man, but for the Lord God. Now with all my ability I have provided for the house of my God for the things of gold, and the silver for the things of silver, and the bronze for the things of bronze, the iron for the things of iron, and the wood for the things of wood, onyx stones and inlaid stones, stones of antimony, and stones of various colors, and all kinds of precious stones, and alabaster in abundance. And moreover, in my delight in the house of my God, the treasure I have of gold and silver, I give to the house of my God, over and above all that I have already provided for the holy temple. . . ." Then the rulers of the fathers' households, and the princes of the tribes of Israel, and the commanders of thousands and of hundreds, with the overseers over the work, offered willingly. The people rejoiced because they had offered so willingly, for they made their offering to the Lord with whole heart, and King David also rejoiced greatly. (1 Chron. 29:1–3, 6, 9)

Tenet Number Four

Leaders must acknowledge the absolute sovereignty of God over the entire universe. God is the creator and owner of all things in the visible and invisible world.

The biblical basis:

> In the beginning God created the heavens and the earth. (Gen. 1:1)

> The earth is the Lord's, and all it contains, the world, and those who dwell in it. For He has founded it upon the seas, and established it upon the rivers. (Ps. 24:1–2)

Tenet Number Five

Responsible financial management is inclusive of developing believers who are good stewards of their personal financial resources. Therefore, the church must not only practice sound management, it must teach it as well.

The biblical basis:

> The rich rule over the poor, and the borrower becomes the lender's slave. (Prov. 22:7)

> No one can serve two masters; for either he will hate the one and love the other, or he will hold to one and despise the other. You cannot serve God and mammon. (Matt. 6:24)

> On the first day of every week let each one of you put aside and save, as he may prosper, that no collections be made when I come. (1 Cor. 16:2)

Tenet Number Six

Leaders are to teach the centrality of missions and ministry.

The biblical basis:

> And Jesus came up and spoke to them, saying, "All authority has been given to Me in heaven and on earth. Go therefore and make

disciples of all the nations, baptizing them in the name of the Father and the Son and the Holy Spirit, teaching them to observe all that I have commanded you; and lo, I am with you always, even to the end of the age." (Matt. 28:18–20)

For there was not a needy person among them, for all who were owners of land or houses would sell them and bring the proceeds of the sales, and lay them at the apostles' feet; and they would be distributed to each, as any had need. (Acts 4:34–35)

So then, while we have opportunity, let us do good to all men, and especially to those who are of the household of the faith. (Gal. 6:10)

NOTES

1. John R.W. Stott, "The Epistles of John," *The Tyndale New Testament Commentaries* (Grand Rapids: William B. Eerdmans Publishing Company, 1983), pp. 224–26. There is a lot about the controversy between John and Diotrephes that is not known. However, whatever it was, it caused a serious problem within the church. Evidently, something of this nature was more than likely known throughout the region.

2. W. E. Vine, *Vine's Expository Dictionary of New Testament Words* (Peabody, Mass.: Hendrickson Publishers), p. 849.

3. See for instance, John F. MacArthur Jr., *The Master's Plan for the Church* (Chicago: Moody Press, 1991), pp. 179–95. Also, Alexander Strauch, *Biblical Eldership: An Urgent Call to Restore Biblical Church Leadership,* (Littleton, Colo.: Lewis and Roth Publishers, 1986). The approach that both men take demands a serious examination of how we look at leadership.

4. MacArthur, op. cit., p. 183.

5. Ibid., p. 183.

6. James H. Harris, *Pastoral Theology: A Black-Church Perspective* (Minneapolis: Fortress Press, 1991), p. 81.

7. Harris, ibid., p. 81.

Chapter Three

The Duties of Church Leaders

*"He is also head of the body,
the church. . . ."*

—Colossians 1:18a

The management of the financial resources of the church is a cooperative effort involving the pastor and several church leaders. The pastor is not solely responsible for the management task alone. However, the pastor should never totally relinquish the responsibility of financial management and accountability to someone else. The pastor should never be afraid to take the mantle of leadership in the area of church finances. In far too many instances, the pastor allows other leaders to make ministry decisions based upon their belief that lay people run the church. When the pastor allows others to determine what the church can and cannot afford to do, he has ceased to be the pastor.

JESUS CHRIST, HEAD OF THE CHURCH

The New Testament makes it clear that Jesus Christ is the Head of the church. In his letter to the church at Ephesus, the apostle Paul wrote, "And He put all things in subjection under His feet, and gave Him as head over all things to the church" (Eph. 1:22). Every leader in the church is subject to the headship of Christ. As Head of the church, the church draws its life and energy from Jesus Christ, who supplies the entire body. It is in Him that we are to grow up (see Eph. 4:16).

The church is a living organism of which Jesus Christ is the Head. The concept of the church as a living organism is based upon the teachings of 1 Corinthians 12. In that chapter, the church is compared to a human body made up of a variety of parts, each having a specific function. A body is not an institution; rather it is a living organism. The point of the passage is to teach that the body is not composed of one member, but many. Paul spoke about the various gifts given to members within the body (see 1 Cor. 12:8–12). The gifts were to be used for the purposes of building up the body (see 1 Cor. 12:4–7). There is a definite spiritual hierarchy established in 1 Corinthians 12:28–30 within the church's leadership structure.[1]

> But now God has placed the members, each one of them, in the body, just as He desired. And if they were all one member, where would the body be? But now there are many members, but one body. And the eye cannot say to the hand, "I have no need of you"; or again the head to the feet, "I have no need of you. . . ." And God has appointed in the church, first apostles, second prophets, third teachers, then miracles, then gifts of healings, helps, administrations, various kinds of tongues. All are not apostles, are they? All are not prophets, are they? All are not teachers, are they? All are not workers of miracles, are they? (1 Cor. 12:18–21, 28–30)

THE ROLE OF THE PASTOR

The pastor is the chief overseer of the church (see Acts 20:28). His office is divinely ordained by God (see Eph. 4:11). He is the person responsible for ensuring that the church is properly led, which includes the management of its resources. The New Testament clearly places spiritual authority within the office of the pastor. One of the tasks Paul gave Titus was to correct deficiencies in Crete. "For this reason I left you in Crete, that you might set in order what remains, and appoint elders in every city as I directed you" (Titus 1:5).

As the overseer, bishop, elder, pastor, or whatever title one wishes to use, the pastor is leader of every facet of the church's life. He is over everything; this includes every office and every activity. He does not, however, do everything; it's an insecure leader who tries to do it all by himself, not trusting others to help (see Exod. 18:13–27).

It is the central task of the pastor to provide spiritual leadership in every aspect of the church's life. He has to interpret to the congregation the vision that God has given him. How the church spends its money is a reflection of its support and confidence in his leadership and God's direction. Therefore, the pastor must possess a clear and concise understanding of the principles of sound financial management. The following is a list of responsibilities that belong to the office of the pastor in the ministry of financial management. He is the chief administrator.

Pastor's Responsibilities
1. The pastor establishes a program of instruction to teach financial money management to the church's leaders and congregation. This is especially true as it relates to the financial management of the church's money.
2. The pastor develops, implements and coordinates the overall financial operation of the church in conjunction with the church business manager, treasurer, chairman of the trustees, financial secretary and deacons. This includes, but is not limited to, the implementation of quality control procedures that safeguard the church's money and financial assets.
3. The pastor ensures that the church's financial officers exercise their fiduciary responsibility in accordance with the church's bylaws and standard accounting and business practices.
4. The pastor prepares annual ministry recommendations for the new year and presents them to the budget committee for inclusion in the annual church budget. He appoints and guides the budget committee in the assembly, preparation, and presentation of the annual church budget.
5. The pastor reviews from time to time the procedures that are followed for receiving, counting, depositing, spending and accounting for church funds. He makes recommendations or receives recommendations from the treasurer, trustees, finance committee, or budget committee for changes necessary to ensure the proper safeguarding and management of the church's assets.

6. The pastor ensures that the proper financial reports are prepared by the financial secretary, treasurer, or church accountant. He leads in the presentation of the reports to the church's leaders and to the congregation.
7. The pastor reviews the overall financial condition of the church. Along with the responsible leaders, he makes the necessary recommendations for implementation in the overall managerial scheme of the church.
8. The pastor ensures that all expenditures are in accord with the proposed spending plan of the church. He consults with the budget committee to make midyear adjustments or changes to the proposed spending plan.
9. The pastor meets with the treasurer, chairman of the trustee board, chairman of the deacon board, chairman of the budget committee, financial secretary, and church accountant to discuss and review the financial condition of the church. These persons are responsible for keeping the church informed as to the financial health of the church. The pastor leads the other church leaders in ensuring that the financial assets of the church are properly managed and safeguarded.

THE ROLE OF CHURCH TRUSTEES

There is no biblical mandate or authority for the establishment of the office of church trustee. However, trustees should be selected using the same criteria and standard for selecting other key leaders in the church. In fact, it would be in the best interest of the church to use the same criteria used for the selection of deacons (see 1 Tim. 3: 8–13). The fact that trustees are not mentioned in Scripture does not eliminate the need nor necessity for their presence.

In many states the law does not require churches to incorporate. An incorporated nonprofit organization, such as the Urban League, United Way, or the American Cancer Society, is required to have a board of directors to run the organization. In states that do not require incorporation, provisions are made for the establishment of a group of people to serve as the legal representatives of the church. These persons are referred to as trustees.

In many churches trustees are viewed with contempt and scorn. There are a number of churches that have eliminated their office and gone to a single board made up of the pastor and deacons. Further, there is in many instances a rift between the pastor and trustees, often over control and power. This need not be! It should not be. The reason that there is this constant battle between the pastor and trustees in many churches is the lack of training regarding the role of the church trustee.

When properly selected and trained, the chairman of the trustee board can be the pastor's most valuable ally in the management of the church's resources. He or she can serve to generate support for the pastor's vision and leadership. It is absolutely unthinkable to consider managing a church without trustees.

Trustees cannot be held individually liable for any of the church's debts or obligations, unless they acted outside the authority of the church. Hence trustees serve the expressed interest of the congregation. They have no legal or spiritual right of control over the church's property or its financial assets. They are not empowered to act on their own. As a body of leaders they have only the authority invested within it by the congregation. The congregation always retains the right to overrule any recommendation or decision made by the trustees.

Most states require that at least three persons be designated as legal representatives of the church. In Virginia there is a requirement for only three persons so designated by official church vote and resolution. If you are not familiar with drafting the resolution designating the official representatives of the church, the local circuit court clerk's office can provide the information and samples. These three persons are approved by the church in a regularly scheduled or annual church meeting. It is not necessary, as some have believed, to have every member of the trustee board registered as legal representatives. The resolution is prepared by the church clerk and sent to the Clerk of the Circuit Court of the city or county in which the church is located. The persons so designated are the only persons authorized to convey church property, sign for and encumber the church in debt, and handle other legal affairs as the church may have.

Given the current state of our economy, society and the highly complex financial world in which we live, it is essential that trustees be better trained. This training should include vital areas of financial management, physical plant maintenance, safety and security, risk management, food service management, personnel management, church accounting, federal and state tax codes, city and state building codes, zoning requirements, etc. Listed below are a list of duties that are the minimum for church trustees.

Trustees' Responsibilities
1. Trustees serve as legal representatives of the church. They make recommendations to the church regarding the retention of legal counsel in matters where counsel is needed. They are the official representatives of the church in all matters involving litigation.
2. Trustees hold the title and deed to all church property. This in no way gives trustees ownership or control of the church's property. They are responsible for safeguarding the legal documents that attest to the church's ownership of property and equipment.
3. Trustees sign all legal documents relating to the purchase, sale, mortgaging, or rental of church property. Only those persons registered with the Clerk of the Circuit Court are required to sign. The trustees are the only persons authorized to sell and buy property on behalf of the church. They sign all contracts on behalf of the church.
4. Trustees are responsible for ensuring that the property of the church, its buildings, grounds and equipment are maintained in an operable condition. They are charged with securing the necessary supplies and equipment to maintain the buildings and grounds. Trustees are responsible for the maintenance of all office equipment and furniture belonging to the church.
5. Trustees are responsible for conducting an annual inventory and survey of the church's property to determine its condition and to check for losses. They are responsible for conducting a fire and safety audit of the buildings and grounds. They should prepare adequate fire evacuation plans and ensure that the plans are properly displayed and known. Trustees should inspect all fire and safety equipment to ensure that it is operable.

6. Trustees are responsible for the risk management plan of the church. They should periodically review and update all church insurance policies to include fidelity bonds.

7. Trustees should be familiar with the local zoning codes that impact the church. They should stay abreast of all property transactions in the community. They should be watchful for opportunities to purchase additional property on behalf of the church.

8. Trustees should be knowledgeable of all the state and federal tax codes and how they impact the church. The trustees should be familiar with reporting procedures, forms, due dates, and deposit procedures and locations for all state and federal filings.

9. Trustees are responsible for ensuring that the church complies with the state and federal equal opportunity laws.

10. Trustees should be familiar with various types of endowment programs, long term investment strategies, procedures for developing long term financial objectives and plans. It is necessary that they be knowledgeable of financial markets and investment strategies to ensure the long term financial viability of the church.

11. Trustees should be familiar with the church's personnel and general policy files.

12. Trustees are responsible for the proper disposal of all church property that needs to be discarded.

13. Trustees must work in concert with the pastor, deacons, treasurer, and the financial secretary to ensure the proper management of all the church's property and money.

THE ROLE OF DEACONS

The deacons have no major responsibility in the day-to-day financial management and administration of the local church. However, there are some churches that have a single board structure under which the deacons function as both trustees and deacons. The primary responsibility of the deacons is to care for the church's membership and to assist the pastor in the conduct of the church's ministry.

In many churches, deacons have come to see themselves as church overseers, whose primary task is to safeguard and run the church. Alexander Strauch has written what I consider to be one of the foremost recent biblical examinations of the office addressing this very issue:

> In many churches, deacons act more like corporations executives than ministering servants. In direct contradiction to the explicit teaching of the New Testament and the very meaning of the name, *deacon*, which is "servant" (*diakonos*), deacons have been made the governing officials of the church. Even more troublesome is the fact that deacons are often placed into a competitive role with the shepherds of the local church. This practice is a proven formula for prolonged church warfare.[2]

I am in no way trying to trivialize or minimize the office of the deacon. Deacons should be kept abreast of the financial affairs of the church. They are one of two biblical offices of the church (see Phil. 1:1; 1 Tim. 3:1–13). The deacons of the church are not responsible for counting the Sunday receipts. When they engage in that type of work, they remove themselves from their true mission and ministry. It must be noted that deacons can serve, and should serve, as members of the committee that counts the church's receipts.

Indeed, the New Testament church deacon, when he exercises his true calling and sure election, is an important person in the ministry of the local church. The work of the deacons is described in Acts 6. Their functions have never changed and should not be changed by churches who want to appeal to a contemporary mentality. Strauch has stated very clearly the role of the church's deacons:

> Through the deacons, the local church's charitable activities are effectively organized and centralized. The deacons are collectors of funds, distributors of relief, and agents of mercy. They help the poor, the jobless, the sick, the widowed, the elderly, the homeless, the shut-in, the refugees, and the disabled. They counsel and guide people. They visit people in their homes. They relieve the suffering. They comfort, protect, and encourage people, and help to meet their needs. In contemporary language, they are the congregation's social workers.

In the New Testament, deacons are always in close relationship with the shepherds of the church. Like the shepherds, they are required to meet specific qualifications. Like the shepherds, they must be officially examined and approved before they can serve. Like the shepherds, they hold an official position of trust in the congregation. Unlike the shepherds of the church, however, deacons do not teach or govern as part of their position. They are servant-officers who relieve shepherds of the multitude of practical duties that are required in caring for a congregation. The offices of overseer and deacon are separate but complementary. The shepherd-elder must give their primary attention to leading the people. The deacons must give their primary attention to caring for the people's physical welfare.[3]

THE ROLE OF THE CHURCH TREASURER

The office of the church treasurer is very important. The church cannot function effectively without a treasurer. The treasurer should be a person of high moral and spiritual character. Here again, the same criteria used for selecting deacons and trustees should be applied in selecting church treasurer.

The treasurer should be a man or woman who has his or her own financial house in order. He should be well organized, possess good people skills, and be someone who is willing to follow the leadership of the pastor of the church. He should not be anyone who has a history of spiritual rebellion or non-support of the church financially. He should be a person who can be trusted with the most sensitive financial information. He must not be talkative. The treasurer should be someone who recognizes that the church's money belongs to God. He must never claim control or dominance of the church's bank accounts or other financial assets.

The treasurer should be familiar with basic church accounting and financial record keeping. He should read various publications that deal with church accounting.[4] For the sake of internal control the treasurer should never be given total control of the church's finances. Listed below are several duties of the church treasurer. It must be remembered that different publications prescribe different duties to the church treasurer. Each church can decide for itself what the responsibilities of the treasurer should be. The list below is one that I feel is the best for maintaining internal control of the church finances.

Treasurer's Responsibilities

1. The treasurer is the chief custodian of all church funds and bank accounts. He or she deposits all funds in church approved banks and institutions.
2. The treasurer opens and closes accounts as the church deems necessary.
3. The treasurer maintains an inventory of the church's safe deposit box in the church safe at all times.
4. The treasurer receives the offerings, turns them over to the counting or finance committee, receives from the committee the weekly receipts, verifies the count, verifies the weekly deposit, deposits the weekly receipts in the bank, and maintains a record of all deposits made by the church. The treasurer may or may not serve as chairman of the finance or counting committee.
5. The treasurer ensures that all church checks and official finance records are maintained in a secure file at the church.
6. The treasurer renders periodic reports to the pastor, deacons, trustees and church at its regularly scheduled business meetings.
7. The treasurer maintains a record of all receipts and expenditures.
8. The treasurer is one of three persons authorized to sign checks drawn on church bank accounts. The treasurer should only write checks in an emergency, when the financial secretary is not available.

THE ROLE OF THE FINANCIAL SECRETARY/ACCOUNTANT

The financial secretary or church accountant is the heart and soul of the church's financial management system. The financial secretary provides all of the financial information needed to make informed and sound decisions. The financial secretary should possess basic bookkeeping skills and accounting knowledge. The financial secretary should possess the same character requirements as the treasurer.

Given the highly technological age in which we live, the financial secretary should be computer literate. It is becoming increasingly necessary for churches to use automated accounting systems to increase efficiency and accuracy. In some cases, the work performed by the financial secretary may be performed by an accountant. Listed below are duties of the financial secretary.

Financial Secretary's Responsibilities

1. The financial secretary maintains all of the financial records, including all bank statements, bank accounts, investment accounts, scholarship funds, and miscellaneous funds for the church.
2. The financial secretary records and maintains a record of the individual contributions of each member of the church.
3. The financial secretary assigns each member a membership number.
4. The financial secretary orders, inventories, and issues each member a set of offering envelopes for their giving.
5. The financial secretary maintains a record of all church current, fixed and long term (mortgages) debts.
6. The financial secretary writes all checks approved by the pastor or the church's business manager (if the church employs one).
7. The financial secretary maintains on file a current balance sheet and income statement.
8. The financial secretary prepares the monthly payroll for distribution to church employees.
9. The financial secretary prepares all state and federal income tax reports, ensures that the amount is deposited in the bank when required, and prepares the necessary W-2 and W-4 forms.
10. The financial secretary prepares quarterly and annual financial reports for distribution to the church membership.
11. The financial secretary maintains the current status of all church bank accounts.
12. The financial secretary prepares a weekly summary and report of all current and fixed debts to be paid.

13. The financial secretary orders church checks and ensures their security.
14. The financial secretary performs other tasks related to the position that may be assigned by the pastor.

THE CHURCH BUSINESS MANAGER

The church business manager is the pastor's assistant when it comes to church administration and financial management. The demanding schedule of the pastor and the many different tasks that require a lot of his time necessitate that he be assisted by others. If there is no church business manager, the pastor serves as the church's business manager.

The business manager may be a member of the board of trustees of the church. In the case of very large churches, the business manager may be someone who is employed full time in the position. The business manager should be someone who *can* and *will* work closely with and for the pastor. If he is not a member of the church, he should be someone who is trained in business and financial management. Prayerful consideration should be given to selecting the church's business manager. If possible, he should be trained or have experience in the area of church or nonprofit organizational management. The business manager should be willing to be trained by the pastor on how the church functions and operates. It is crucial that the business manager understand that the ministry is always central and takes precedence.

The church business manager works under the leadership and supervision of the pastor. He is the pastor's right hand in all matters that relate to the day-to-day financial administration of the church. The pastor may, if he so desires, relinquish to him the authority to approve certain expenditures. These are things that relate to auxiliary programs and day-to-day operations. In the absence of the pastor, however, the authority for approving church expenditures is the chairman of the trustee board.

The church business manager may or may not be a member of the church budget committee. He is the person designated to authorize purchases in accordance with the church's annual budget. He works with the budget committee and financial secretary to ensure proper administration of the church's budget. The business manager should render periodic reports to the trustees regarding church business operations. The authority of the business manager never exceeds that of the pastor or the board of trustees of the church.

The business manager should from time to time review budgetary and spending procedures and make recommendations to the pastor regarding changes. The business manager may be charged with supervising the work of the financial secretary.

THE FINANCE COMMITTEE

The finance committee is composed of persons approved by the church for the purpose of counting weekly church receipts. They may or may not be church officers, i.e. deacons or trustees. The committee is under the direct supervision of the chairman of the committee or the church treasurer. The committee is responsible for opening, verifying, and counting all monies received in the weekly church offering. The committee is responsible for preparing the necessary deposit forms and turning over the verified deposits to the church treasurer for deposit in the church's accounts. All church monies should be counted immediately following the worship service. Counting during the hour that worship is taking place dishonors the Lord and sends the message that money is more important than the Word of God.

THE BUDGET COMMITTEE

The budget committee is responsible for preparing the annual church budget of proposed income and expenditures. The committee reviews the previous year's budget, makes recommendations for changes, and receives from the pastor his annual list of ministry recommendations to be funded. The committee receives from each auxiliary its proposed budget request for the year.

The budget committee has no regulatory power or authority. The committee makes recommendations to the pastor for changes to be made to the budget, during the course of the year. The committee monitors the expenditures of the church to ensure that spending is in accord with the church's budget. The committee works with the pastor to establish a date for a congregational hearing on the budget, for the purpose of receiving comments and suggestions for the proposed annual church budget.

NOTES

1. The question of Paul's intention for listing the various offices in numerical order is beyond the scope of this effort. I recognize that the issue must be viewed against the backdrop of the schism in the church over spiritual gifts and Paul's particular place among the church's leaders. There are several good sources who are much better qualified to shed light on the subject and the reader is recommended to see them: C.K. Barrett, "The First Epistle to the Corinthians," *Black's New Testament Commentary* (London: Henrickson Publishers, Inc., 1968); Gordon D. Fee, "The First Epistle to the Corinthians," *The New International Commentary on the New Testament* (Grand Rapids: William B. Eerdmans Publishing Company, 1987); John MacArthur, "1 Corinthians," *The MacArthur New Testament Commentary* (Chicago: Moody Press, 1984).

2. Alexander Strauch, *The New Testament Deacon: The Church's Minister of Mercy* (Littleton, Colo.: Lewis and Roth Publishers, 1992), p. 9.

3. Ibid., pp. 156–57.

4. There are a number of good publications available that will help church treasurers to grasp their work. See for example: Thomas E. McLeod, *The Work of the Church Treasurer*, rev. ed. (Valley Forge, Pa.: Judson Press, 1992); Jack A. Henry, *Basic Accounting for Churches: A Turnkey Manual* (Nashville: Broadman and Holman Publishers, 1994); David R. Pollock, *Business Management in the Local Church*, with a foreword by Larry Burkett (Chicago: Moody Press, 1992); Daniel D. Busby, *The Zondervan Tax and Financial Guide: Church and Nonprofit Organization, 1996 Edition* (Grand Rapids, Mich.: Zondervan Publishing House, 1995).

Chapter Four

The Functions of
Money Management

*"And they received from
Moses all the contributions
which the sons. . . ."*

—*Exodus 36:3*

One of the foremost dangers that faces the local church is the mismanagement and misappropriation of its money. Scandals have developed in churches over money because of leaders who were too trusting and created an environment for money to be taken. Or they have given too much authority and responsibility to one person, without any internal checks and balances.

Every church should periodically review its internal money management procedures. This includes everything that happens to the offering once it is placed within the plate until it arrives in the place designated for counting and is eventually deposited in the church's bank account. In terms of financial money management, this is called internal control. Mack Tennyson has defined internal control this way, "It is a checks and balances system to prevent stealing."[1] Without proper checks and balances the church leaves itself open for the possibility of mismanagement. That is not to say that those who count the church's money are to be viewed with suspicion.

People who count the church's money must be among the most trustworthy and reliable people in the congregation. They should not be people who are experiencing personal financial problems. It becomes too easy to take the church's money, as a means to make up for personal financial shortfalls.

THE FUNCTIONS OF INTERNAL CONTROL

Tennyson has identified four things that internal control does for the church.[2] First, it makes it difficult for anyone to steal the church's money. In case you don't know it, people have stolen money from the church. I have friends who have had to deal with thefts of church funds. It is important that we not create a situation wherein the church's money can be stolen. Many churches have lost money by theft from long standing members and officers because they did not consider theft as a possibility.

Second, internal control removes the snares and traps that give rise to the theft of money. I remember once preaching a revival for a friend. After the offering was lifted, one man would come and gather the offering plates and leave alone with the money. It would be a while before he would return. This church was too trusting and it created a situation in which the man could have taken small sums of cash and it never be missed. I am in no way saying that this is what happened. In all things we should avoid the very appearance of evil by not giving people a reason to have suspicions. At least two or three people should escort the offering from the sanctuary.

Third, internal control reduces errors in the accounting of church funds. All monies should be counted at least twice and verified by someone other than the person counting and a record should be made of the count.

Fourth, internal control protects the treasurer and the persons charged with counting the church's money from week to week. Even experienced committees and treasurers can make a mistake. Sound internal controls will catch counting or deposit errors before they happen. The last thing any church wants to have is a credibility problem for its leaders who count the church's money.

THE FUNCTIONS OF MONEY MANAGEMENT

According to Jack A. Henry, there are four distinct functions of money management. They are receiving, recording, budgeting and spending.[3] All of these functions are central to the efficient and sound management of the church's money and other assets. I am going to take a brief look at these functions in this section. More will be said about budgeting and spending in later chapters.

RECEIVING MONEY IN THE CHURCH

Money comes to the church regularly. In some churches money arrives daily or there are activities that take place where money is either collected or brought to the church. There should be some system in place to receive and account for these funds. When Moses was commanded by God to build the Tabernacle money had to raised (see Exod. 25:1ff). During the construction process the people brought their financial gifts daily.

> And they received from Moses all the contributions which the sons of Israel had brought to perform the work in the construction of the sanctuary. And they still continued bringing to him freewill offerings every morning. (Exod. 36:3 NASV)

Thomas E. McLeod has identified several sources from which money can be received during the week:[4]

1. Offering collected during regular worship services.
2. Offerings collected from Sunday School and Bible Study.
3. Weekly suppers, banquets, and other occasions with meals.
4. Mail receipts that come to the church during the week.
5. Occasional sale of books and literature to members.
6. Special fund-raisers such as the sale of bonds, etc.

Every church should examine its procedure for how funds from various sources are received and safeguarded until they are deposited in the bank. If sound internal controls are not in place to protect the money and the persons handling it, then they should be immediately instituted.

The Sunday Offering
The church trustees should ensure that a plan is in place to protect the weekly offerings and the church's treasurer from suspicion. One

of the most difficult rumors to kill are the ones about money being missing from the church's accounts or unexplained errors in the records.

Many churches have multiple services on Sunday. At each worship service an offering is taken. These funds need to be safe-guarded and handled the same way. There should be at least two persons always available to receive and put funds away until the time for counting the offering has arrived. As a matter of security there should never be a time when church receipts are in the hands of just a single person, unsecured. Some people put loose cash in the offering. How this is handled has to be a concern for church leaders. It is very easy to misplace cash.

The committee counting the church's weekly receipts should always do its work at the end of the worship service. God is not honored when money is taken out during the worship and those who count it miss the preaching of the Word of God.

There should be internal controls for those who are counting church receipts. Care should be taken to assign two persons to count and verify each specific collected fund, i.e. building fund, operating fund, scholarship fund, etc. Each church should design a form that can be used by the counting committee to report and verify the weekly receipts. The form should be signed by both persons counting that particular fund and verified by the church's treasurer, who signs as well (see Figure 4-1).

Most churches use some form of envelope system. One person should open and verify the amount written on the envelope. The other should count the money. If the amount written on the envelope and the actual amount is different it should be corrected immediately and reported to the treasurer for verification. If the amount in ques-tion is large, then the person should be contacted immediately and informed of the situation. Whatever system is used should be clearly understood by all who are members of the counting committee.

When money is received during the week, it should either be deposited within twenty-four hours or locked in a safe or file cabinet, with very limited access, usually by two or three persons. All funds received during the week should be recorded and a record made of the date and amount received. This will protect the office staff or whoever opens and receives the mail.

```
┌─────────────────────────────────────────────────────────────┐
│                                                               │
│                     Weekly Finance Report                     │
│                   Main Street Baptist Church                  │
│                        Anywhere, U.S.A.                       │
│                                                               │
│                                                               │
│     Date_____                                        │
│                                                               │
│                                                               │
│     Tithes_____│
│     Building Fund_____│
│     Missions Fund_____│
│     Public Offering_____│
│     Auxiliary Gifts_____│
│     Other_____│
│     Total_____│
│     Counted By:_____│
│                                                               │
│                     _____  │
│     Verified By:_____│
│                                                               │
└─────────────────────────────────────────────────────────────┘
```

Figure 4-1. Weekly Finance Report

RECORDING MEMBERSHIP GIVING

It is vitally important to adopt a program whereby the church can keep an accurate record of the giving of its membership and visitors. The weekly or periodic contributions of the membership represent the single largest source of revenues for the church. In the Word of God there are numerous references to the people of God supporting the work of the Temple or the first century Christian church (see Exod. 36:1–7; Lev. 27:30–32; 1 Chron. 29:10–14; Hag. 1:1–6; Mal. 3:7–12; Luke 6:38; Acts 20:35; 1 Cor. 16:2; 2 Cor. 9:6–7).

In order to accurately account for the individual contributions of members and visitors, each member should be assigned a membership number. Most of the offering envelopes available today come with numbers pre-assigned. This enables the financial secretary to keep an accurate record of the member contributions. In addition to assigning envelope numbers to members, it's a good idea to establish a file for visitors who are regular supporters of your church's ministry. This will make it easier to send each visitor an end-of-the-year letter thanking them for their contributions. It will also enable the financial secretary to provide them with an official statement to file with their federal and state income taxes. Visitors to your church will thank you for it.

COMPUTERIZED ACCOUNTING

Advances in technology have led many churches to become auto-mated. The use of computers in the accounting and record keeping of the church has many benefits. First, computerized record keeping increases efficiency and saves time in preparation of church financial statements and reports. Second, it increases the accuracy of the reports. Third, it enables the pastor and leaders to have up-to-date financial information. Fourth, it reduces the time and work hours needed to prepare membership contribution statements. Fifth, the church can print multiple checks in a matter of minutes, while the computer simultaneously records the information in its general ledgers and accounts files. It is difficult to think of operating effi-ciently without the use of a computer.

However, there are a great number of churches that have not gone to the use of computers. I remember when we purchased our first system in 1984, the question was raised, "What are we going to do with a computer?" I had no personal experience in their use. In fact, I did not even own a personal computer. Yet, I knew that in order to keep abreast of our growing membership, to increase efficiency, and to maintain accurate records, it was necessary that we move in that direction. Now the church owns four personal computers, which contain all of our records and perform a variety of functions.

A word of caution is due here. If you are not familiar with the use of personal computers, the first thing you will need to do is educate yourself. You will need to learn the language and technical jargon used in the computer industry. It may be helpful to take an introductory course in the basics. The second thing you will need to do is determine your needs. What functions do you want the computer to perform? Third, you will need to spend time shopping around to find the best equipment for your money. Many personal computers come loaded with all kinds of software programs that you may not even need. Fourth, look for the appropriate church software that will meet your needs. Here again, there are a number of products on the market. Talk to your local religious supply store representative or Baptist Bookstore manager about software products. Talk to other pastors who have led their churches in computerizing their records, and get their recommendations. This will save you a lot of time and frustration. Fifth, invest in training your staff in the proper use of the equipment and software. It will be money well spent. See Figure 4-2 for several software vendors that sell software exclusively for churches.

1. Church Information System
   127 Ninth Avenue North
   Nashville, TN 37234
   1-615-251-2247

2. F1 Software
   208 Ridgefield Drive
   Asheville, NC 28806
   1-800-486-1800
   1-704-665-7799 FAX

3. Parsons Technology
   One Parsons Drive
   Hiawatha, IA 52233
   1-800-957-3111
   1-319-393-1002 FAX

Figure 4-2. Sources for Financial Software

GIVING AND THE IRS

In 1993, the U.S. Congress passed the 1993 Federal Tax Act. The Act required that all contributions over $250 must be accompanied by a written statement from the charitable organization to which the money was given in order for the donor to claim it as a deduction on their income tax returns. The new ruling took effect on December 31, 1993.

For individuals who tithe, problems can be created without the record. I learned how important it was to have church documentation during an IRS audit several years ago, prior to the passage of the law. During an audit, several of our family's financial contributions were disallowed because I could not produce church records of our contributions. In today's political climate the IRS will disallow all contributions which do not have proper documentation from the church.

The statement of giving provided to each member or visitor can be mailed to the IRS along with their tax return, saving them the frustration of an IRS audit. Jack Henry stated that:

> When the tax return is "flagged" by the IRS computer for audit because of the large amount of charitable giving that is deducted, the IRS reviews the actual return. When they see that the deduction is valid, they will likely stop the audit process if there are no other reasons to call for an audit.[5]

Accurate accounting of contributions will save the church and the members embarrassment during tax reporting season. Regardless of the time that may be involved in keeping accurate records of individual contributions, it will be money and time well spent. If there are differences between the member's records and church's records, a reconciliation should be done immediately to correct it. The church should retain member contributions envelopes on file for a minimum of eighteen months. This will allow time for any questions regarding contributions to be researched and thoroughly answered.

THE ANNUAL AUDIT

The financial records of the church should be audited annually, either by an internal auditing committee or by an outside accounting firm. In cases where the church is relatively small, an internal audit by qualified church members may be sufficient. However, even small churches should, from time to time, have their records audited by an outside accounting firm.

In the case of large churches, there should be an annual audit of the church's financial records by an outside accounting firm. This may seem unnecessary to some people. However, given the intense scrutiny of church finances and the billions of dollars that flow through church accounts each year, I feel it's a necessity. This will say to the world that the people of God have nothing to hide.

According to David R. Pollock, "an audit is an honest, objective, and impersonal evaluation of the church's financial systems and procedures and its financial statements."[6] When an audit is properly performed, it will result in the detection of accounting and recording errors, deficiencies in church policies, and gaps in internal control.[7] Pollock gives five advantages of an audit.[8]

1. It helps to improve the church's financial reporting systems, procedures, and internal control.
2. It can result in suggestions for improvement of systems and procedures.
3. It can help a church avoid potential financial and legal problems.
4. It can result in improved church operations.
5. It provides assurance to the congregation and outsiders that the church's financial records are being properly maintained.

Further, he suggests that churches try to find an individual or a firm that specializes in nonprofit organizations when looking for an outside auditor.[9]

For many pastors, money management is a nightmare. However, it does not have to be. Any pastor who is willing to take the time, make the effort, and expend the energy can learn how to design a money management system for his church. There are a number of basic resources on the market that are geared primarily to churches and nonprofit organizations. When we demonstrate faithfulness and a commitment to honesty, God is glorified and the church will feel that it has leaders with integrity.

NOTES

1. Mack Tennyson, *Church Finances for People Who Count: A Basic Handbook for Church Treasurers, Trustees, Deacons and Ministry Staff* (Grand Rapids, Mich.: Zondervan Publishing House, 1990), p. 51.

2. Ibid., p. 32.

3. Jack A. Henry, *Basic Accounting for Churches* (Nashville: Broadman and Holman Publishers, 1994), p. 8.

4. Thomas E. McLeod, *The Work of the Church Treasurer,* rev. ed. (Valley Forge, Pa.: Judson Press, 1992), p. 17.

5. Henry, op. cit., p. 29.

6. Pollock, *Business Management*, p. 59.

7. Ibid., p. 58.

8. Ibid.

9. Ibid., p. 59.

Chapter Five

Developing and Administering the Church Budget

*"Now with all my ability I
have provided for the house
of my God. . . ."*

— *1 Chronicles 29:2*

Very few pastors look forward to the budget preparation and approval cycle that comes every year. Usually, this is the time of the year that the pastor has to justify his existence and his vision to people who may have no idea of what God is trying to do through him and the church. The period in which the budget is being prepared may be especially painful if the church has had to deal with financial shortfalls during the course of the year. I contend that financial management, of which budgeting is a part, does not have to be a battleground. When church leaders are properly trained to understand the basics of church fiscal administration and accountability, it makes the pastor's job a lot easier.

The planning of a church's budget is really a very exciting and wonderful time of the year. During this period the church has an opportunity to seriously evaluate every aspect of its ministry and program. It has an opportunity to assess the effectiveness of its services and staff. The church has an opportunity to reward faithful employees. The period that the annual budget is being prepared gives the church an opportunity to discontinue ministries and programs that are not meeting any real needs. Lastly, the budget process gives the church an opportunity to forge forward in new areas of ministry and community service.

In this chapter we will take a look at how to organize a budget committee and get the proposed annual budget approved by the congregation, with as little tension as possible. We will also take a look at a sample budget and how it should be organized. There are a number of ways to develop a budget for the church. I am only offering one that I have found to be most effective and least stressful for me and the congregation.

WHAT IS A BUDGET?

A budget is nothing more than a proposed plan for organizing and spending your financial resources. A budget is a plan, and it's always better to have a plan than no plan at all. Jack Henry offers the following explanation of budgeting:

> Budgeting money is simply a matter of setting priorities on everything that you want to do so that the money is used for the most important things *first*. By doing that, no matter how much or how little money you have to spend, you will always do the most important things with your money.[1]

Budgeting is a spiritual, financial discipline. A church's budget is the result of prayer for the guidance and direction of the Lord. It is the product of reflection, planning, organization, and decisiveness. When a church makes and adopts a budget, it has made a conscious and clear decision about what it believes is the will of the Lord for that church.

ORGANIZING THE BUDGET COMMITTEE

The budget committee is one of the most important committees in the church, therefore, careful consideration should be given to its composition. In some very small churches the pastor may prepare the budget alone and present it to the church. Generally, however, this is not the case. There are churches in which just the deacons are members of the budget committee. Then there are churches where the trustees are the budget committee. Still, some churches may empower a finance committee to serve as its budget committee and to oversee finances. None of the above, in my mind, represent a good budget committee. Oftentimes church leaders are more focused on reducing cost and expenditures which can have a negative impact on church growth.

The preparation of the annual budget of the church should never be in the pastor's hand alone, nor in the hands of deacons, trustees, or a finance committee. The committee should be made up of a cross segment of the entire church congregation. A typical committee should consist of between five or seven members: one member from the deacon and trustee boards, the church clerk, various other leaders, and members from the general congregation. No member of the committee should serve more than two to three years. By limiting the length of time a person may serve, it opens up the process for more people to be involved in charting the financial course of the church.

The committee should be selected and trained by the pastor. Churches will sometimes stipulate in their bylaws that the budget committee is appointed by some church legislative body, which is just an attempt to limit the pastor's input and direction. The pastor knows the members who love the Lord and the church. He knows the members who will put the Lord's work ahead of any personal agenda. Without the pastor's personal input in determining who constitutes the committee the work of the church could go in a direction totally different than the Lord intends.

According to Jack Henry there are four implied questions related to the budgetary process:[2]

1. How much money will be available to spend?
2. What needs to be done?
3. How much will it cost to accomplish each need?
4. What is the order of priority among the things that need to be done?

My experience has been, and I am sure it has been yours as well, that church spending decisions are notoriously difficult to make, primarily because we tend to operate from a pool of limited resources which are always determined by the previous Sunday's offering. Therefore, there is hardly ever enough money available to do all that needs to be done when it needs to be done. This makes the church's budgeting and spending plan all the more crucial. Without a sound budget and spending plan, the church will simply drift through financial cyberspace, not knowing where it is headed.

THE BENEFITS OF A CHURCH BUDGET

When the church takes budgeting seriously, several benefits will result.

1. Budgets force churches to take planning seriously.
2. Budgets are a way of involving everyone in the church in the decision-making process.
3. Budgets enable a church to think about its future and the direction it wants to go.
4. Budgets enable churches to project into the future and provide resources for future infrastructure and ministry needs.
5. Budgets are a very useful tool for resource and cash flow management.
6. Budgets provide the means for anticipating staff increases by providing the necessary salary and benefits ahead of time.
7. Budgets enable the church to seek new and innovative ways to be used by God for greater ministry and service.
8. Budgets determine spending limits and provide the means by which cash flow is effectively managed.
9. Budgets challenge the membership to responsible giving.

THE ROLE OF THE PASTOR

The pastor is the central person in the development of the annual church budget. I say that because the pastor is *the leader* of the church. He is the one whom God has called to provide spiritual direction for His people. The pastor is the one whom God has given the vision. As the congregational leader the pastor cannot be afraid to share the vision that God has given him, nor the costs that are associated with achieving the vision. The pastor sets the tone and climate for the church, not the followers. During the time that the church is developing its annual budget, the pastor must be boldly committed to the

vision God has given him. He is the shepherd of the flock. He must
provide the leadership that will take the church where God intends.
Robert D. Dale writes of the pastor's leadership role:

> Pastors must be congregational leaders. Fortunately, we aren't
> the only leaders in our churches. But we must provide leader-
> ship in the congregation. It goes with the territory. Generally
> defined, leadership is an action-oriented, interpersonal influ-
> encing process. In essence, leadership involves vision and
> initiative. More comprehensively, pastoral leaders see visions of
> ministry, communicate our dreams clearly, gain consensus and
> commitment to common objectives, take initiative by setting the
> pace in ministry actions, and multiply our influence by trans-
> forming followers into new leaders. Pastoral leaders differ from
> church managers. Church managers conserve and concentrate
> on doing things right; pastoral leaders create and focus on doing
> the right things.[3]

The pastor, therefore, leads the church's leaders, the budget
committee, and the congregation in the planning, adoption, and
implementation of the church's budget. He embodies the dreams and
direction of the church.

TYPES OF BUDGETS

There are several types of budgets that can be used by a church or
any nonprofit organization. For our purposes we are going to take a look
at the two that are most frequently used, the "line-item budget" and the
"ministry-action budget." This will not be a detailed discussion, because
there are a number of publications available on church budgets.

Line-Item Budget
The line-item budget is a list of items, services, ministries, positions, and programs that are listed in the budget. Each item is
assigned some dollar amount, based upon a projection made by either
the pastor, the budget committee, or the leader whose group will

Missions and Outreach		
National Missions		$1,200.00
State Missions		1,000.00
Local Missions		500.00
	Total	$2,700.00
Christian Education		
Church School		$2,500.00
Library/Materials		1,500.00
	Total	$4,000.00

Figure 5-1. Line-Item Budget

receive the funding. Dale asserts that the line-item budget calls attention to the different totals spent rather than the ministry that is carried out.[4] Figure 5-1 is an example of a line-item budget format.

Ministry-Action Budget

Ministry-action budgeting is a form of budgeting that begins with evaluation and justification. That is to say, each ministry or program or expense is evaluated annually. During the evaluation process, it may be discovered that a particular ministry or program is no longer meeting any needs within the congregation or community. When the committee formulates the budget, that particular program or

Our Missions Ministry and Outreach		
Foreign Missions		$3,500.00
Home Missions		2,500.00
Local Missions		2,000.00
State Convention		4,000.00
	Total	$12,000.00

Figure 5-2. Ministry-Action Budget

ministry can be completely eliminated and the church's resources allocated in other areas (see Figure 5-2). Dale states, "Each organizational unit begins without any funding, proposes its activities for the next year, costs out every proposed ministry action, and then prioritizes each of its decision packages for committee and congregational consideration."[5]

DEVELOPING THE BUDGET

The preparation of the annual church budget is a decisive process. It is decisive because budgeting involves making decisions about the future direction of the church over a specified period of time. A church budget should not be something that is painstakingly developed over the period of a few days. Rather, it should involve a whole series of evaluations of the ministry of the church. Henry states:

> What many people consider to be 'budgeting,' that is the action of listing things to be bought or paid for and what each costs, is only one of the activities of the budgeting process. Budgeting also includes setting goals, assigning priorities to them, developing a plan for achieving them, operating the plan, evaluating the results, and replanning.[6]

According to Henry, there are several things that must take place before the budgeting process is complete.[7]

1. Set goals for the year.
2. Establish priorities for each of the goals.
3. Estimate your income for the year.
4. Estimate your expenses.
5. Balance the Budget, or get the projected expenses equal to lower than the projected income.

Each of these activities are part of a deliberate effort to envision and interject God's will and purposes into the spending plan of the church.

Set Goals for the Year

Goals are those *specific* and *achievable* tasks that the pastor wants to lead the church to accomplish during the course of a year. Church goals are the product of the shared vision of the pastor and the people. As the pastor shares God's vision with clarity, the people will see and take hold of the goals, making them their own.

Goals must be specific, that is they should not be some general idea that does not apply to anything. A church goal may be to reduce its debt. A more specific goal is to reduce its debt by a specific amount during the year. For example, one goal may be to reduce the church's mortgage debt by $3,000.

Goals should be achievable, that is, the goals should not be tasks or things that are outside of the possibility of the congregation. The pastor may believe that what he proposes is entirely within the realm of possibility. However, his congregation may not be mature enough or ready to make that great a leap of faith. In the example above, reducing the church's debt by $3,000 may be achievable, while on the other hand, reducing it by $10,000 may be totally unrealistic. The resources of the people and the church may be inconsistent with the goal.

Establish Priorities

Priorities are the tasks that must be accomplished first. They are the most important jobs that you want to see accomplished during the year. They should be listed in descending order, with the most important priority first. Everything that is to be done is not of equal importance. There will be some things that you would like to do; however, they should not be assigned a high priority. Priorities grow out of the church's goals for the year. One church goal may be to reduce the church's debt, a second may be to purchase an updated computer system, a third goal may be to replace the leaking roof. In terms of priorities, the roof replacement must be given the highest priority. The other two can be assigned a place based upon the values of the congregation.

Estimate Your Income

Establishing a realistic budget for the year must be based upon—using as close an estimate as possible—your church's projected income. There is nothing magical or scientific about estimating income. It is based upon looking at the current and historical financial information of the church, and establishing a historical pattern of growth and giving.

The pastor should be assisted by the budget committee in developing an estimate of projected income. Listed below are the steps for making an estimate of your church's income.

Step One: Be open to the leadership of the Holy Spirit and seek new ministry possibilities for your church. In Proverbs 3:5–6 we read, "Trust in the Lord with all your heart, and do not lean on your own understanding. In all your ways acknowledge Him, and He will make your paths straight." The Holy Spirit will never lead us astray.

Step Two: Review all of the records of the past four quarters to determine the church's income. Pay specific attention to months or weeks when income was high and when it was low. Note any special appeals or unusual one-time offerings or gifts. Often, these gifts are not taken into consideration when projecting income.

Step Three: Calculate the average increase or decrease in giving for the previous three, five and ten year periods. This enables you to formulate a realistic growth history of the church. There may have been some unusual circumstances contributing to either increases or decreases in income.

Step Four: Calculate the rate of membership growth during the same periods, i.e. three years, five years, and ten years. This will enable you to see the relationship between the church's numerical growth and the growth of giving during the period.

Step Five: Determine from the weekly financial reports what the average weekly offering has been for the previous six quarters. Performance over the previous six quarters gives a much clearer picture of where you have been and what you have done. Remember, in the church, things often move very slowly, so that what is voted on in one year may not be implemented for another twelve to fourteen months.

Step Six: Make a list of all of the possible sources of income: tithes, public offerings, building fund, renovation fund, missions fund, special gifts, Sunday School, revivals, anniversaries, men's day, women's day, dinners, book sales, audio and video tapes.

Step Seven: Make allowances for unusual circumstances that can reduce projected income. One of the factors that impacts giving is weather. In areas where members rarely see much snow, it is important to anticipate the possibility that snow can close the church during the winter. There must be some consideration given to the possibility that an area could be hit by a hurricane, if you live in hurricane regions.

Step Eight: Don't forget, when you are raising money for new construction, it tends to reduce giving to other church causes, such as missions or debt liquidation. Many members may not increase giving for these efforts, but rather they will redirect what they presently give.

Step Nine: Always be conservative in your estimates. If your historical growth patterns reflect a rate of growth of 12 percent, base your estimate of future growth at 6–8 percent. This enables you to project for growth, but it also allows you to factor in the possibility of economic downturns or reductions in giving.

Guidelines for Estimating Expenses

After you and the committee have come up with a reasonably sound estimate of projected income, you then must estimate your expenses, including the cost of operating and missions and ministry efforts you wish to fund during the year. Listed below are several guidelines that may be helpful in estimating your expenses.

1. Always begin your estimated expenses list with your missions, education and ministry. If you identify physical

plant and salaries as first, you establish that as your main priority. The members of the church will generally follow the lead of the pastor. A number of pastors make the tragic error of thinking that by reducing their missions and educational expenses, they will raise more money quicker for a building project. The church merely kills its dream when it de-prioritizes missions and education.

2. Always be liberal in estimating your costs. It's better to be way over than to underestimate the cost of operating. Assume that the worst can happen, as it usually does.

3. Always list your fixed costs after your missions, education, and ministry costs. These are going to remain constant. For instance, if the church has a mortgage, it definitely has to be paid. Salaries and benefits are another category of fixed costs.

4. Always include a category for the church's endowment. One of the fallacies of many church administrators is the failure to financially plan for the church's future. If your congregation is not comprised of well-to-do people who can bequeath the church a great deal of money, then you must plan for the future. One way is to include it as an item in the budget. It's fine to leave coming generations a great spiritual legacy, but in this current economic environment, there is a need for more ministry resources. In Proverbs 13:22a, "A good man leaves an inheritance to his children's children. . . ."

Balance the Budget

The budget should balance. Projected expenses and projected income should be equal. A good church budget should be one that reflects the pastor's vision, has been cooperatively constructed, contains specific goals, uses the best conservative estimates, balances expenses and income, and is achievable by the congregation.

GETTING THE BUDGET APPROVED

During the latter half of 1995 and into 1996, the President of the United States, William Clinton, and the U.S. Congress were at odds over the national budget. The Republicans wanted certain social programs removed from the budget, thereby reducing expenses and cutting the budget deficit. The President, on the other hand, was committed to his agenda and to keeping many of the social programs in place that, he believed, would have a devastating impact on the poor and elderly if they were cut.

As a result, the President and the Congress were unable to agree on a budget for the country. The government was shut down, federal workers were furloughed without pay, and the whole nation was forced to wait out the squabbling between the President and the Congress. Without an approved budget there could be no real direction or plan for spending the taxpayers' money. The leaders of the free world were trapped by their own pettiness.

Budget approval time in the average church is a "tedious and tasteless hour." Many pastors dread this period like the plague. It always seems to bring out the worst in people. I believe that part of the reason for difficulty in getting the budget approved is the process that is followed. If there is a cloud of secrecy about the pending budget, it tends to give the people the feeling that someone is trying to hide something, or put something over on the church.

One of the other reasons many pastors dread the budget process is that during the approval process they see church leaders in a different light. Any discussion about salary increases will always be met by opposition from some church leaders. There are church leaders who may live for the purpose of denying the pastor any leadership in the area of church finances. New and badly needed equipment, new programs, staff increases and many of the internal things that are needed to make the church's ministry more effective are sometimes met with hostility and rejection. For many pastors, the fear of constant rejection of progress kills their motivation and thirst for innovation in the church. The church becomes stagnant because the pastor has lost his desire to fight.

I want to suggest a method for getting the church's budget approved. It will not guarantee total success, but it may make the process less painful. The process that I am suggesting takes between four to six months. If followed, with modifications for your particular church, it should make budget approval a high time in the church.

STEPS TO A SUCCESSFUL BUDGET

Step One: The pastor, prayerfully, appoints the members of the budget committee and sets an initial meeting date. At that time he appoints the chairman of the committee and discusses the agenda for the first meeting.

Step Two: At the first meeting, the pastor conducts a study of church budgeting. *Basic Budgeting for Churches: A Complete Guide,* by Jack A. Henry would be an excellent resource to use. It's simple and straightforward. The pastor continues to meet with the committee until they have completed a study of the textbook.

Step Three: The pastor meets with the budget committee. At this meeting the pastor discusses with the committee the current financial situation of the church. The committee should have before it all of the financial statements of the church, i.e. quarterly income statements, balances sheets, and complete journal listings, if they are available. The committee conducts a complete evaluation of the church's spending for the past year. Special consideration is given to evaluating church revenue sources and establishing giving and spending patterns.

Step Four: While the budget committee is conducting its review of the church's financial records, the pastor presents his vision for the coming year to the church's leaders. He shares with them all of the things that the Lord has laid upon his heart for the coming year. Each of the leaders is encouraged to share the vision with his group members. The pastor does not ask the leaders for a vote on his vision at this meeting. The entire church will have to decide whether or not it will adopt his vision for the future. Further, at this session the pastor has members of the budget committee instruct the leaders, in small groups, on how to complete the budget request form (see Figure 5-3). They also provide instruction to leaders on the church's financial operation, i.e. how to request funds, the importance of meeting submission deadlines, and record keeping procedures.

First Baptist Church
1998 Budget Request Form

Ministry Requesting Funds_____

Group Leader_____Date_____

Amount Requested_____Date Submitted_____

Purpose of Funds_____

_____

_____

_____

Dates that funds will be needed_____

_____

Amount Approved_____Date_____

Reason for Denial/Reduction_____

_____

_____Chairman

_____Pastor

Figure 5-3. Budget Request Form

Step Five: The pastor presents his vision and spending proposals to the budget committee. He discusses with the committee their order of priority. At this time, the committee receives from the church's boards and group ministry leaders their individual budget request forms. The committee, along with the pastor, establishes a priority expenditure list from all of the submitted requests. The committee continues to compile the request forms and begins to assemble the church's budget.

Step Six: The pastor meets with the budget committee and presents his proposal for employee salary and benefit increases. If the church has a personnel committee, the pastor meets with them to discuss employee salaries and benefits. The personnel committee then submits to the budget committee a proposed salary package for all church employees for the coming year. The personnel committee should never present recommendations to reduce any church employee's salary. Final approval for any salary-related matter must always come before the church.

Step Seven: The budget committee presents the first draft to the pastor for review and discussion. The pastor reviews the proposed budget and makes any changes he deems necessary.

Step Eight: The pastor presents the budget to the deacons for their comments. He then discusses it with the trustees to receive their comments. After the two boards have had a chance to review the budget, the pastor convenes a meeting of all of the church's key leaders or pastor's council to review and discuss the proposed budget. At this meeting the leaders review, discuss, and recommend changes to the proposed spending plan. After discussion, the pastor entertains a motion that the proposed budget, with changes and recommendations, should now proceed to the congregation for review, discussion and final approval.

Step Nine: The pastor meets with the budget committee to discuss the results of the meeting with the key leaders of the church. At this meeting the pastor establishes a date for a congregational budget hearing. The committee ensures that the budget is distributed to every member who wishes to receive a copy. Usually it is best to do this on a Sunday. The pastor announces to the congregation the process by which the church will review, amend and approve the church's annual budget.

Step Ten: The chairman of the budget committee, along with members of the committee, meet at the designated hour to receive concerns or recommendations from the congregation. The committee answers any questions raised by members of the church. The pastor only speaks if there is a need for him to answer questions that are referred directly to him. The annual budget hearing is conducted entirely by the budget committee. If the pastor has properly done his work, there is no further need for him to say anything. Usually, at the budget hearing only a few people will show up, unless there is some hot issue to be discussed.

Step Eleven: Those that meet with the overall objective and mission of the church are included in the budget and given a priority listing. Those that do not meet the church's objectives are turned down and the member is informed, by the chairman, of the reason for the committee's action. The pastor sets the date to vote on the annual church budget after all of the procedures have been followed.

Step Twelve: The pastor leads the church in voting on the proposed budget. At this meeting there is no further discussion of the budget; each member votes for it or against it. Generally, by now there has been so much discussion and review that there is rarely any public opposition to the proposed spending plan.

MANAGING CASH FLOW

Preparation, presentation, and approval of the annual budget is not the end of the budgeting process. There has to be constant monitoring and evaluation to ensure that the church stays on track with its spending plan. Once each quarter or bi-monthly, the budget committee should meet and review the income and expenditures. The committee should report to the pastor and the church regarding spending goals. The committee should make recommendations to the pastor for adjustments to the budget as the year progresses.

The day-to-day management of the church's cash, its expenditures and the internal control procedures for requesting funds is done by the pastor or the church business manager. In some churches, the trustees may designate one of its members to work with the pastor in this area.

Date_____Voucher No._____

Check No._____

Check Requested by_____

Please issue check to:_____

Amount of check_____

Purpose of check_____

_____

Charge to Account No._____

Return check to:_____

Pastor's Signature_____

*Chairman of trustees signs in pastor's absence.

Figure 5-4. Funds Request Voucher

It is important that a well defined procedure be in place for requesting funds (see Figure 5-4). Further, it is important that leaders understand the process and comply with it.

Developing a church budget and managing the financial resources of the church does not have be a complicated and involved process. The process merely needs to be organized with clearly defined lines of authority and responsibility. There are a number of resources available to assist the pastor and church financial officers with setting up proper financial records.

Within the local church, the pastor has to be allowed to provide the necessary oversight and leadership of the church. Clearly, this means that he must be chief financial administrator of the church. He should be assisted by men and women who are able, not greedy, nor possessed with domineering spirits. The pastor must be given the latitude to delegate financial management responsibilities to other leaders. No one person can successfully lead a church by himself.

The pastor must be secure and confident enough in himself that he is not intimidated by men and women who can bring spiritual insight, strong leadership, and managerial skills to their task of managing the church's money.

We must all remember that our success is tied to the ability of those under us to succeed in what they are doing. Their failures will ultimately lead to ours. Nowhere is this more evident and apparent than in the management of the church's money. Efficient and effective management of the church's money leads ultimately to a successful ministry.

NOTES

1. Jack A. Henry, *Basic Budgeting for Churches: A Complete Guide* (Nashville: Broadman and Holman Publishers, 1995), p. 6.
2. Ibid.
3. Robert D. Dale, *Pastoral Leadership: A Handbook of Resources for Effective Congregational Leadership* (Nashville: Abingdon Press, 1991), pp. 13–14.
4. Ibid., p. 119.
5. Ibid.
6. Henry, op. cit., p. 14.
7. Ibid.

————— Chapter Six —————

Paying the Pastor and
the Church Staff

*". . . The laborer is worthy
of his wages."*

—*1 Timothy 5:18*

In September, 1980, I accepted the call to become the pastor of my first church. I was full of excitement and was thrilled that I was going to finally get an opportunity to pastor a church. It was doubly exciting because I was still a seminary student. Among my peers I had achieved a measure of success. I had someplace to preach every Sunday. There was no longer any need to wonder about where I would spend the next Sunday. I was a pastor. I knew where I would be. What a great feeling! It did not matter that the church was located eighty-five miles from Richmond, Virginia, where I went to seminary. We would all just have to get up early on Sundays and leave home in time enough to arrive for Sunday School, which began at 8:45 A.M.

When I was initially interviewed by the deacons, I was asked if I would be willing to move to the small rural county. I could hardly wait to graduate from seminary nine months later and move into the parsonage that the church owned.

The parsonage, built in 1927, was in need of extensive repair. My wife was horrified when the chairman of the deacon board took us on a tour of the home. The church had done very little work on the property. Rosetta was simply shaken by its appearance and total inconvenience. I, on the other hand, did not see any of the problems that my wife saw with the parsonage. All I saw was the opportunity to be pastor of the church.

62

Unfortunately, nothing prepared me for the shocking reality of being a servant of God, and I felt like a mortal slave. The church paid me a very meager salary which included nothing for health insurance, life insurance, retirement, transportation, conventions—nothing. All we had was a house built in 1927 and a $200 a week salary. Occasionally, some of the members who were farmers would leave a basket of fresh vegetables on the front porch for us. Those were indeed some very difficult times for us. My salary was so low that my daughter qualified for the school lunch program.

Every year there would be a big discussion among the church leaders about the pastor's salary and how much of a raise he should receive. It was a bit embarrassing for me. I was not quite sure how to handle the situation. The courses I had taken in seminary never prepared me for negotiating salary and benefit packages. After all, when I was in the Army I never had to worry about medical bills, retirement or pay raises. The government took care of those things. I felt like the Apostle Paul, "O wretched man that I am! who shall deliver me from the body of this death."

After a year of living under very adverse conditions, I decided that I would have to move. I could not convince the people to pay me more, and the renovation job they did on the parsonage was a real waste of the church's money. I preached for several vacant churches and inter-viewed with them. During one interview I was asked by a member of the pulpit committee, "Reverend Guns, what kind of salary do you expect to receive?" My response to him was, "Certainly, more than I am now receiving." Needless to say, I was never invited back to preach. During the same period, I was a candidate for the vacant pulpit of the church I currently serve. When I interviewed with the church, they made me what I considered to be a far superior financial offer than what I was currently receiving. The church offered a salary that was in effect about the same as I was receiving at my current church. However, at Second Calvary, they were prepared to provide a complete benefit package, which was something I had not previously had. I am indebted to my predecessor. He taught the church how to provide a salary and benefit package for the pastor. I must point out that the salary, while not great, was the start of a new beginning for us.

By the time I moved on from my first church to Second Calvary, we were so deep in debt and so broke, that it would take us from 1983 until 1988 to turn things around. Our furniture was old and dilapidated. The two cars we owned were in a sad state of disrepair. Our wardrobes were tattered and in need of replacement. My story is probably the same as that of many pastors, young and old.

Churches tend to be very poor employers. I do not mean poor in terms of money, but rather in terms of how they treat and take care of their employees. How the church is going to compensate its pastor, ministry support staff and other workers is a problem. As Bramer has pointed out:

> A substandard minister's salary is often explained away by referring to the adage that the minister must serve out of a sense of call, and that his concern for the material well-being of himself and his family must be subrogated for his love of work and desire to serve the kingdom.[1]

There are several reasons why churches are poor employers. First, church leaders have not been trained to understand what constitutes an adequate compensation package for a minister. What is the pastor worth to the church? Often many of the people who are making decisions regarding the salary and benefits of a pastor or professional staff have no idea of the cost for professional degrees. Seminary is a three-year commitment, which is the length of time it takes to earn a law degree or some other professional degree. Further, the people who make these decisions may see the pastor as being overpaid if he is fairly compensated, based upon his worth to the church.

Second, preachers tend to be their own worst enemy when it comes to speaking up for pay and salary packages. Sometimes we are so happy to be preaching that we will take whatever the church offers. There is this pious and naive notion that "the Lord will provide." The Lord does provide. He provides through the people we serve. The pastor must become his own best advocate, training his leaders on how to fairly and justly compensate himself and other staff workers. He must not be afraid to share with his leaders his financial needs and situation. Manfred Holck Jr. has expressed the dilemma of poorly paid pastors quite well.

> Far too many congregations have actually failed to take their responsibility seriously. In addition, too many pastors, fearful of

antagonizing members or reluctant to express overt concern about money matters, have failed to confide in trusted members about the actual circumstances of their financial needs. As a result, congregations have assumed that the pastor's compensation was adequate, while pastors, frustrated in their desire to serve the congregation competently, have fretted about their ability to make ends meet. In the face of inflation's dramatic impact on costs, some clergy families are simply unable to cope.[2]

Third, churches that employ bi-vocational pastors tend to be relieved of a lot of the responsibility for providing an adequate salary. Pastors who have a full-time day job may not want to burden the church with paying them. They may feel that it would be wrong to ask the congregation to provide more, and some of the members may think the preacher is greedy. The preacher who is bivocational needs to be aware that one day someone else will follow him. If he remains until retirement, the church will have an anemic view of what is fair compensation. Even a bi-vocational pastor works full-time. There is no such thing as a part-time pastorate.

THE DRAWBACKS OF UNDERPAID PASTORS AND STAFF

Just think for a minute how it feels to be underpaid. Now you have an idea of how the pastor and church staff must feel. Underpaid pastors and church staff have a negative impact upon the church and its ministry. Listed below are several drawbacks that the church experiences when it underpays its pastor and staff.

1. The church never reaches its fullest potential because it never calls the best, most capable person to serve the congregation. Everything is money driven, which interferes with sound decision making. It costs a little more to get better qualified preachers and staff. Low pay keeps away the best candidates and drives good ones to other churches.
2. The pastor and staff are not as productive as they could be. When the pastor or other church workers have to worry about money, it distracts them, keeps their mind on their personal financial plight.

3. The pastor is never in a position to retire. Because the church does not pay enough, the pastor may not be able to save for retirement. He has to stay at the church until he is either asked to leave or dies of old age at the church. The members become tired of him and he of them, yet he cannot leave, because he is not financially able.

4. The church is always in transition. When the church is calling a new pastor every five to seven years, it leaves the congregation in disarray and unable to grow properly. The period between one pastor leaving and the new one arriving is the worst time for a church. Churches rarely grow or make any progress. It's best to pay a living salary and keep the pastor and staff in place.

5. When the pastor and staff are adequately compensated the incentive to remain with the church is present. There is no incentive to remain when the bills are past due and the parsonage has bad plumbing. The incentive to perform at a peak level is gone when workers are not paid properly and have no benefit program.

UNDERPAID AND OVERWORKED

The average pastor works very hard and is underpaid. David R. Pollock cited a compensation study done by the National Association of Church Business Administration in 1991 that revealed the extreme disparity of the salaries of ministers.

> A recent study points out that the average American pastor with a congregation of three hundred people earns a salary of $17,875. One out of five ministers moonlights to supplement his income. In fact, one study done ten years ago indicated that only 5 per cent of American ministers earn more than $22,000 a year, and 14 per cent earn less than $10,000.[3]

Low clergy pay is not restricted by denomination nor race. There is an equally disparate number of African-American clergy who are poorly compensated by congregations that they serve. In a major study released in 1994 of the Black Church in America, C. Eric Lincoln and Lawrence H. Mamiya found that black clergy continue to have problems in the area of salaries. "The median income for rural clergy was in the $10,000 to $15,000 range, while urban clergy reported a median income in the category of $15,000 to $25,000."[4] Clergy income is lowest in rural areas. However, even many urban pastors are faced with low pay and no benefits or allowances for retirement, health or any other type of insurance.

The pastor is never free from work. His days are perpetual. While a day off may be ideal, the reality is if there is a family crisis, funeral, hospital emergency, wedding, or some other church related function, he is expected to be present. If he leaves for any of the major holidays, Christmas, Mother's Day, Easter Sunday, New Year's Day, the members may frown with disapproval. Given the enormous work load of the pastor, it is only fair that he be compensated adequately.

PAY THE PREACHER : IT'S IN THE BIBLE

The Word of God speaks directly to the requirement that the people of God provide for those who serve them in spiritual matters. The Law of Moses provided that the Levites, who were responsible for the services at the Tabernacle, were to be taken care of by the people. Because of the nature of their work, they were excluded from receiving an inheritance when Israel divided up the promised land (see Num. 3:5–13; 8:14–22; Deut. 18:1–8). They were to receive a portion of the offering brought to the Tabernacle for their support. The law also provided that the Levites were to begin serving at the age of twenty-five and retirement was mandatory at age fifty (see Num. 8:24–26).

The apostle Paul had to deal with the matter of compensation for preachers of gospel during his ministry. It was of particular concern to the Corinthians, who obviously had a problem with compensation for Paul. In his first letter to the church he provided clear instruction. In 1 Corinthians 9:3–14, we have the clearest statement in the New Testament regarding the responsibility of the church to provide for the preacher's welfare. Gordon D. Fee remarked that in the passage Paul defends his right for material support from the Corinthians.[5]

My defense to those who examine me is this: Do we not have a right to eat and drink? Do we not have a right to take along a believing wife, even as the rest of the apostles, and the brothers of the Lord, and Cephas? Or do only Barnabas and I not have a right to refrain from working? Who at any time serves at his own expense? Who plants a vineyard, and does not eat the fruit of it? Or who tends a flock and does not use the milk of the flock? I am not speaking these things according to human judgement, am I? Or does not the Law also say these things? For it is written in the Law of Moses, "YOU SHALL NOT MUZZLE THE OX WHILE HE IS THRESHING." God is not concerned about oxen, is He? Or is He speaking altogether for our sake? Yes, for our sake it was written, because the plowman ought to plow in hope, and the thresher to *thresh* in hope of sharing *the crops*. If we sowed spiritual things in you, is it too much if we should reap material things from you? If others share the right over you, do we not more? Nevertheless, we did not use this right, but we endure all things, that we may cause no hindrance to the gospel of Christ. Do you not know that those who perform sacred services eat the *food* of the temple, and those who attend regularly to the altar have their share with the altar? So also the Lord directed those who proclaim the gospel to get their living from the gospel.

There are several key thoughts that are important for us to understand from the passage.

1. The servant of the Lord is sent by God to serve God's people. The proof of his ministry is the fruit of his labor among those whom he serves. (verses 1–2)
2. The servant of the Lord has a right to have a family and to provide support for them. (verse 5)
3. The servant of the Lord has a right to serve the Lord full-time. Just as soldiers, farmers and shepherds reap from their work, so does the servant of the Lord. (verses 6–7)
4. The Lord has provided in the Word that even animals are to be compensated from the source of their labor, how much more should his servant be. (verses 8–10)

5. The sowing of spiritual seed blesses the people; therefore, the people bless the servant of the Lord through their material things. (verse 11)
6. If creditors, who provide no spiritual blessings, have a claim upon the people of God, how much more should the servant of God have a claim for the good he does. (verse 12)
7. The servant of God lives by the preaching of the gospel. (verses 13–14)

Double Honor

Pastors who work hard, give unselfishly of themselves, spend long hours in study to prepare for the teaching and preaching ministry should be doubly compensated. A central question is, "how much is the preacher worth to the church?" The Bible answers the question with clarity. Nowhere is the answer made clearer than in Paul's first letter to Timothy. I am amazed that many Bible believing deacons and trustees are very quick to hold up the standards of 1 Timothy 3:1–7, but fail to hold up the requirements of 1 Timothy 5:17–18. "Let the elders who rule well be considered worthy of double honor, especially those who work hard at preaching and teaching." For the Scripture says, "You shall not muzzle the ox while he is threshing" and "The laborer is worthy of his wages." Let's take a closer look at this matter of "double honor" and its implications for paying the pastor and the church's staff.

The word "elder" refers to someone who leads and presides over the church. Paul pointed out three functions of the church elder.

Figure 6-1. Functions of an Elder

Ruling (*proistemi*, Greek) in the sense that Paul used it, refers to everything involved in leading, guiding, administering, overseeing and shepherding the flock. The distinguishing factor among elders is performance. Those who "rule" are counted worthy of honor, but those who do it well are to be considered worthy of "double honor." They have earned the double honor based upon their performance. As D. Edmond Hiebert has stated regarding elders who rule well, "Such honor is their due and the congregation should not be remiss in this matter through their failure properly to express their appreciation for his work."[6]

Preaching (*logos*, Greek) is not used in the original text, but rather the statement reads, "those who labor in the Word." As Strauch has pointed out, "The context, which is the primary consideration for translating a term with such a broad range of meaning, demands the rendering 'preaching' in a general sense such as in exhorting, admonishing, gospeling, and comforting."[7]

The apostles considered the "ministry of the Word" to be their primary calling (Acts 6:2, 4). They learned the importance of preaching from Jesus, who preached the gospel of the Kingdom of God (Matt. 4:23; 9:35; Mark 1:14–15, 38). Jesus commanded that those who follow Him would go into all the world and preach the gospel (Mark 16:15ff; Acts 1:8; 2:14ff; 5:42).

The elder who works hard at preaching is to be considered worthy of double honor. It is in the preaching of the gospel that the church is edified. Preaching inspires the saints who are experiencing difficulty. The members of the church can tell when the pastor has really spent time before the Lord and the Word, seeking a word just for them.

Teaching (*didaskaliai*, Greek) refers to the act of instructing, with the intent of building up, convincing, and exhorting. Teaching is central to the life of the church. Jesus taught and commanded that His disciples go into all the world teaching, as well as preaching (Matt. 5:1ff; 28:18–20). The early church spent many long hours teaching (Acts 2:42; 11:26). The ability to teach was one of the qualities sought in an overseer of the church (1 Tim. 3:2).

Teaching is hard work and everyone is not capable of teaching God's Word with clarity, simplicity, and with illuminating power. In fact James 3:1 warns that not everyone should take up the ministry of teaching. In order to teach effectively, the teacher has to spend many long hours in study and preparation. Someone suggested to me that I could easily prepare my sermons on Saturday night in about an hour. Clearly, this kind of baseless thinking is reflective of a lack of knowledge concerning what is actually involved in preparing to preach or teach God's Word. Preaching begins with study.

When the church is blessed with a pastor who is an excellent leader, biblical teacher, and preacher, then he is worthy of double honor. He is worthy of being paid very well. Further, if he is lazy and does not provide sound leadership, he should receive nothing. He is more of a hindrance than he is a help. This should be true for church staff workers who work hard in their particular ministries.

Double honor (*diple time*, Greek) has presented some interpreters with a problem regarding how to understand what Paul meant. It is clear that he was referring to how the pastor is compensated. Warren W. Weirsbe has translated the words to mean, "generous pay."[8] The word "honor" might be translated to mean "honorarium" or "stipend." The pastor is worthy to be paid generously for the many hours of work he puts in strengthening and building up the body of Christ. The most obvious question at this point is what should the pastor and church staff be paid? In the next section, we will take up the question of how to construct a wage and benefit package for the pastor and other full-time employees of the church.

THE PASTOR'S SALARY PACKAGE

It's time to determine the pastor's salary and the salary of church employees, and it's the same old story, year end and year out. "How much are we going to pay the pastor and the church's staff?" As Bramer has pointed out, " In most churches the determination of the salary for the minister must run the gauntlet of church boards comprised of members with varying economic backgrounds, so that any given time the salary may be considered too high, too low, or just right."[9]

The pastor and church staff have no privacy when it comes to their salaries. Everyone in the church is privileged to the information. It's a matter of public record. The church budget is widely distributed among the church's membership. All it takes is one disenchanted key leader to throw the whole process into chaos. In many cases, the pastor has to sit and listen to people debate whether or not they think he deserves a raise or an allowance for retirement or transportation.

Churches have used and tried a number of methods to determine what ought to be the salary and benefit package given to the pastor and church staff. Some churches will conduct extensive studies of the salaries and benefit packages of comparable size churches in their region. The information is assembled, evaluated and some values are assigned and a median is used to determine the pay of church employees. I am not sure that this is an effective and fair way to pay your pastor. There are studies that have been prepared by some denominational offices. It may be helpful to check with your denominational office to see if there is information available that addresses salary and benefit packages.

Each church needs to develop its own method, without being influenced by what other churches are doing. I am not suggesting that its not useful to see what others have done. It's always helpful to have a starting point. However, be guided by the spirit of the Lord and His Word and not what other churches are doing. There are four reasons why I believe that each church must make its own determination of what is financially fair.

First, it may be that the churches in your region have never had a good record of being generous in paying preachers. Second, you cannot make comparisons between churches and pastors. Churches are so different, each having a culture all of its own. Third, you make the assumption that your pastor is doing equal work with other pastors in the area. Fourth, churches have different economic levels. A church in the inner-city is not going to have the same financial resources as a church in a middle class or upper class neighborhood. It's always helpful to see what others have done, but it's not always advisable to adopt their models. Each congregation can create a compensation package with the right tools.

The eight factors listed below speak clearly and distinctly (see Figure 6–2). If a pastor has served a congregation continuously for several years, faithfully exercising oversight of the church, and has

---

Considerations for Pastor's Salary Package

Years of Continuous Service
Education and Experience
Leadership Ability
Growth of the Church
Rate of Growth in Giving
Ministry Accomplishments
Public Recognition of the Church
Number and Variety of New Ministries

Figure 6-2. Factors Influencing Clergy Pay

developed the kind of ministry that has led to spiritual growth in the lives of members, he should be so duly recognized. Many times pastors are not recognized for their contributions to the life of the church. You know whether or not the pastor has made a difference in the life of the church. One does not have to be an analytical genius to determine if the ministry of the pastor has made a difference in the life of the people of God. If he has made a difference, then he should be rewarded accordingly, and the church should not make an issue out of it.

Putting the Compensation Package Together
    The compensation package of the pastor should be put together by a small group of church leaders who have spent time in prayer and studying the matter. There are a number of things that must be considered, especially the tax consequences of the compensation package. Many church leaders have no idea of how complicated the returns are for filing federal income tax forms which are related to the ministry. There are a number of preachers who have no clue as to what the IRS requires of them. Too often we will rely on the advice of others, who may not be familiar with the unique issues associated with ministers. There are excellent computer software programs that can be used to determine tax requirements for ministers. These can be

Fiscal Year 1998

Salary	1997	1998	Diff.
Cash Salary	____	____	____
Housing Allowance	____	____	____
Utilities Allowance	____	____	____
Retirement Allowance	____	____	____
Performance Bonus	____	____	____
Other	____	____	____
Total Cash Salary	____	____	____
Fringe Benefits			
Health Insurance	____	____	____
Life Insurance	____	____	____
Disability Insurance	____	____	____
Social Security Allowance	____	____	____
Liability Insurance	____	____	____
Total Fringe Benefits	____	____	
Ministry Costs			
Automobile Allocation	____	____	____
Continuing Education	____	____	____
Conventions	____	____	____
Entertainment	____	____	____
Books/Library	____	____	____
Office Expenses	____	____	____
Ministry Supplies	____	____	____
Other	____	____	____
Total Ministry Costs	____	____	____

Figure 6-3. The Pastor's Compensation Package

secured from your local computer software retailer.

The minister's compensation package should consist of several categories of income. The first category is the cash salary. This is the amount of money that the church actually pays the pastor. The cash salary should not be determined based upon the other benefits given

---

Church Employee Status

<u>Ministry Staff</u>
Cash Salary
Retirement
Convention Allowance
Continuing Education
Housing Allowance
Automobile Allowance
Health Insurance
Group Life Insurance
Disability Insurance
Social Security Contribution
Paid Vacation

<u>Non-Ministry Staff</u>
Cash Salary
Retirement Contribution
Health Insurance
Group Life Insurance
Disability Insurance
Social Security Contribution
Paid Vacation
Paid Holidays (specified)

<u>Part-Time Ministry</u>
Cash Salary
Retirement Contribution (within limits
   of the law)
Social Security Contribution
Convention Allowance
Paid Vacation (after a specified period)

<u>Part-Time Staff</u>
Cash Salary
Retirement Contribution
   (within limits of the law)
Social Security Contribution
Paid Vacation (after a
   specified period)

Figure 6-4. Compensation for Church Employees

to the pastor. The cash salary category includes the housing allowance and housing-related costs.

The second category is the category that includes fringe benefits. Fringe benefits are a very important part of the financial package for the pastor and all church employees. In the pastor's benefit package are such things as an allowance for social security, medical insurance allowance, life insurance, disability insurance, retirement plans, and transportation allowances. An allowance for social security is one of the most important fringe benefits to be given to the pastor. The federal government looks at ministers differently when it comes to paying social security taxes. Ministers are considered to be employees for federal income taxes and are treated as self-employed for social security purposes. The two are very different and have very different tax consequences.

The third category is reimbursements for professional expenses. These include the use of the pastor's automobile in conduct of his ministry, conventions/conferences, books, subscriptions, child care, church-related entertainment, professional dues and memberships, and continuing education. These areas are all different and require a considerable amount of study to understand them.[10] The church should ensure that enough money is set aside to ensure that the pastor attends every major annual meeting of the church denomination.

Tax Considerations

There are a number of tax considerations that should be considered when structuring a salary and benefit plan. Because of the complexity of these rules, I am not going to attempt to explain them. It would take up a considerable amount of time and space. However, these rules can have serious implications for the church and affected employees.

During my first pastorate, I had my income tax return prepared by a professional tax service. The preparer asked me if I had paid estimated taxes during the year. I had no idea what he was talking about. I had only earned $10,200 in salary that year. Because I had not paid any social security, had no qualified deductions, and did not understand the housing rules, we were hit with a $2,500 tax bill. You can imagine that I was totally devastated. First, I had earned next to nothing, then the government wanted 25 percent of my next year's salary.

I strongly recommend that the pastor and leaders become personally knowledgeable of how the IRS Rules impact your church. Many churches are completely out of compliance with the rules simply out of ignorance. The three books that I have listed that refer to taxes are an excellent place to begin. However, I would strongly suggest that you consult with the Internal Revenue Service and a qualified certified public accountant or tax attorney. You may save yourself and the church a lot of heartburn in the future. Church leaders should make every effort to comply with the Internal Revenue Service Code.

Busby has listed the top ten mistakes made by both ministers and churches as it relates to the Internal Revenue Service Codes. The ten biggest tax mistakes made by ministers are listed below.[11] These mistakes can be very costly, as I learned.

Common Tax Mistakes Made by Pastors
1. Filing as self-employed on ministry income for income tax purposes, using tax benefits only available to employees, and leaving yourself vulnerable to reclassification by the IRS to employee status.
2. Failing to have a housing allowance designated when living in a church-provided parsonage.
3. Excluding the housing allowance designated by the church without reducing the exclusion to the lowest of three factors.
4. Confusing the fair rental value of a church-provided parsonage (only includable for social security purposes) with the designation of a portion of your salary as housing allowance (providing an exclusion for income tax purposes).
5. Failing to keep a log of miles driven for personal use vs. church purposes.
6. Claiming an office-in-the-home, a position extremely difficult to support under present law.
7. Not documenting business expenses to reflect business purposes, business relationships, cost, time and place.
8. Failure of employee-ministers (receiving Form W-2) to use an accountable reimbursement plan.
9. Improperly calculating self-employment social security tax.
10. Improperly opting out of social security because you don't think it is a good investment.

Common Tax Mistakes Made by Churches and Other Not-for-Profit Organizations
1. Not setting up an accountable expense reimbursement plan for employees (receiving Form W-2).
2. Providing or adjusting housing allowances for ministers on a retroactive basis.
3. Improperly classifying employees as self-employed.
4. Failure to report taxable fringe benefits paid for self-employed workers.
5. Deducting FICA tax from the salary of qualified ministers.

6. Not reporting taxable fringe benefits, reimbursements for moving expenses, and social security as additional compensation to employees.
7. Failing to file Forms W-2 and 1099-MISC for workers.
8. Providing receipts for the donation of services, rent-free use of property valuing non-cash gifts. Receipting contributions designated for individuals without proper control by the board of the donee organization.
9. Not providing Worker's Compensation coverage where required by law and coordinating Worker's Compensation with health insurance coverage.
10. Failure to comply with the Fair Labor Standards Act for church-operated schools, including day care centers, preschools, and elementary and secondary schools.

HIRING CHURCH MEMBERS AS EMPLOYEES

The question of whether or not a church should hire its own members is very sticky and quite complicated. It is not one that you can easily answer and make everyone happy. If you read ten books on the subject of hiring practices in the church, all ten would probably say it isn't a good idea to hire members. If you were to interview ten pastors, who have had members working for them on the church staff, seven out of the ten would probably agree, it isn't a good practice to hire your members. I wish that there was an easy answer to this question, but there isn't. There are a number of factors that have to be considered when dealing with this matter. That is why every church needs a clearly defined personnel policy that addresses this matter and the relationship of employee to employer.

When I was a college student, my father hired me to clean the church each week. At the time, the church was small and did not have many members. The salary was ten dollars a week. I had to clean the church, keep the leaves raked, and mop and clean the bathrooms. I was thrilled. After all, I could use the money. It was fine for a few weeks. Then I became tired of going every Saturday. Soon my work performance started to suffer. My father called me into his office for counseling. I promised him that I would do better. I did for a few weeks. Soon I was right back to doing the half job I had been doing. The next time my father approached me about my work, he took my keys. Well, it did not take me long to figure out what that meant.

In hindsight, I don't fault my father for what he did. He was the pastor, I was his son. Who would say anything to him about my poor work performance? I can just imagine that he and my mother may have been a little embarrassed at my sloppy housekeeping. I felt relieved. One of the advantages that my father had when he fired me was that there would be no political consequences reverberating through the church at the next church meeting. Every pastor who has ever tried to fire a politically strong member knows of the tumultuous turmoil that it creates. It's not as easy as one might think. Members will make statements like, "We will have to make sure that everyone understands the employee/employer relationship." Often, this idealistic plan fails. I have listed below several factors to be considered when hiring church members to work for the church.

Considerations When Hiring Church Members
1. What kind of support has the member given to the ministry of the church? Has he or she been actively involved?
2. Have they demonstrated a personal relationship with Jesus Christ as their Savior?
3. Do they financially support the church?
4. What is their conduct like in church meetings?
5. Is this person always at the center of church controversy?
6. Do they possess the necessary skills and training for the job?
7. What kind of attitude does the person have?
8. How does the individual get along with the pastor?
9. Do they work well with other members?
10. Do they talk a lot about church business?
11. Is their name ever connected with church rumors?
12. Are they politically active in the church?
13. Who do they talk to most?
14. Are they involved in the church's denominational endeavors?

15. Do they understand how the church operates and is organized?
16. Have they ever demonstrated a thirst for power?
17. What is their church attendance record like?
18. Do they attend Sunday School and other services?
19. How do they work with church leaders?
20. Have they demonstrated that they can follow orders?
21. Can they be loyal to the pastor?

SAVING AND INVESTING FOR RETIREMENT

How many pastors have you known who have spent years laboring and giving of themselves to a church only to retire into poverty? How many times has the preacher's wife and family been asked to vacate the church parsonage after the pastor dies? It happens all too often. Preachers are very poor financial planners. We tend to believe that the people we shepherd will take care of things for us. We tend to want to believe that our best financial interest will be looked after. The reality is that many of our church leaders may not have a clue as to how to make a personal financial plan for themselves, let alone make one for the pastor.

One of the things I say to pastors and young ministers in workshops and seminars is, "plan for your retirement." Don't rely solely on any one plan, nor even a denominational plan. The cost of future retirement is going to be very expensive. Without a consistent savings and investment strategy, the pastor may not be in a position to retire in the future.

Where do you start? You can start by going to your local bookstore and buying some books on retirement planning. Talk to professional financial planners. Make an appointment to meet with several different stockbrokers and discuss retirement planning. Continue to read and educate yourself and your leaders on the subject. Learn about mutual funds, dividend reinvestment plans, government securities, municipal securities, IRA accounts, tax-sheltered annuities, 403(b) plans and how they work, self-employed retirement plans, and all of the other instruments available that you can use to plan for your retirement. One of the best things that any preacher can do for himself and family is sit down with a certified financial planner and develop a personal financial plan. A member of my church told me once, "Reverend, no matter how good you are today, there is going to come a time when the people will get tired of you. You just get old." No matter how well you preach and teach today, there will come a day when you will not be able to function at the same level. Plan for retirement, even if you decide later not to retire. There comes a day when a new generation will not remember your personal sacrifices on behalf of the church.

THE CHURCH AS EMPLOYER

Churches are notoriously poor employers. One of the reasons for this may be the lack of expertise in many churches with fair employment practices. Sometimes we feel that labor relations practices have no place in the Lord's house. After all, we are all Christians. But churches do need to develop personnel policies and procedures for the sake of employees and for the employer's benefit. The Lord expects us to treat our workers fairly and to pay our pastors a living wage. We fail many times to recognize that good employees who love the Lord and His kingdom are not always readily available. Therefore, churches should make every effort to hire and keep all good employees. It is important that we begin to think of equity and fairness in how we treat church employees and how we pay them.

Salaries: The Annual Increase/Decrease

It's November 30 and the budget committee is facing a deadline. It must complete the proposed church budget by December 1. The final items to be determined are the annual salary increases for the pastor and the church staff. I mention the pastor first, because, as a general rule, the salary increases of the church staff will mirror that of the pastor's. During the discussion, the comment is made by a committee member, "The church cannot afford to pay any more than it's already paying." Someone else remarks, "No one offered me the kind of salary and benefits we give our pastor."

Then, at long last, the voice of reason speaks and says, "The church has grown. The pastor has worked hard all year. He has made tremendous sacrifices to help the church grow. He is an excellent teacher and a fairly decent preacher. He has earned a salary increase." Every pastor needs an advocate, someone who will speak strongly on his behalf, when it comes time to compensate him for his work.

In many churches, discussions about the pastor's salary tend to be the flash point for lashing out at the pastor and discussing what some members may consider to be his failures during the past year. Discussions regarding the pastor's salary do no have to become bitter feuds. By simply taking the time to raise the right questions and establishing a fair system of evaluation, these kinds of concerns can be eliminated. It's vitally important that arbitrary evaluation standards are not set up. Churches need to be very careful when they want to establish some criteria for evaluating pastoral performance. Here again the church needs to be guided by spiritually mature persons and those who have a respect for the office of the pastor.

What should be the criteria by which a church determines the starting salary of a new pastor? Second, what should be the criteria or standard that is used to determine the sustaining salary of the pastor and church staff? By sustaining salary, I mean the salary necessary to maintain a decent quality of life. Professional athletes and corporate executives are rewarded based upon their performance. The pastor is not a professional athlete, although at times he runs like one. Neither is the pastor a corporate executive, although he is expected to think like one. There should be an established plan to measure performance. After all, the church grows based upon the quality of leadership, teaching and preaching of the pastor. Good music is fine and quality physical properties are an excellent draw, as are programs of all types. However, people still come to church to hear the pastor preach. Just as Zedekiah asked Jeremiah, "Now King Zedekiah sent and took him out; and in his palace the king secretly asked him and said, 'Is there a word from the Lord?' And Jeremiah said, 'There is!' Then he said, 'You will be given into the hand of the king of Babylon!'" (Jer. 37:17). The members of the church sit and wait for the pastor to deliver to them, Sunday after Sunday, "a word from the Lord."

Determining the Starting Salary

The starting salary for a new pastor, fresh out of seminary, should be the equivalent of one and one-half times the starting salary of a new teacher in your local school district, depending on the size of the congregation. Another method to determine starting salary may be to look at local school administrators, i.e., principals, and use that as a basis for determining the starting salary of the new pastor. Thirdly, a church may call upon its denominational office to get some idea of what should be the starting salary of the new pastor.

In the case of a pastor who is experienced, the church should consider past performance, achievements, education, and perceived abilities. Many churches will make the starting salary the main criterion by which they decide to call a new pastor. The church should do its very best to provide a new pastor with a stress-free salary.

The Sustaining Salary Increase

The sustaining salary increase is the annual salary increase that enables the pastor and church staff to sustain their current standard of living. The church should never reduce the salary of its pastor and staff. It would be far better to reduce the staff than to demoralize the pastor and staff by reducing their salaries.

During the period that our church was raising money for the construction of a new sanctuary, the church staff, along with myself, went three years without any salary increases. The recommendation for such a drastic move came from me. My thinking was, at the time, that by demonstrating personal sacrifice on the part of the pastor and staff, we would raise more money and people would be more supportive of the construction vision. I have since learned that is not the case at all. All you do is plunge the pastor, his family, and the church staff further and further behind the economic power curve. It's not a good idea to fail to reward the pastor and staff for church growth regardless of any major capital improvements that may be taking place. After all, the only reason that the church may be engaged in building is because of the spiritual leadership of the pastor.

Methods for Determining Annual Salary Increases

Annual Growth Method. Take the previous year's growth in church income and membership and use it as the basis for determining the pastor's salary increase. If the church grew by five, seven, or ten per cent, use that as the basis for the determining annual salary increases. This is an excellent incentive for the pastor and church staff.

Average Growth Method. Ascertain the average rate of growth of the church, income and membership, over the past ten years. Take the average rate of growth and use that as the basis for determining the pastor's salary increase for the year. This allows the budget committee to take a long-term view of the pastor's performance. If the pastor has not been at the church for ten years, use the time that he has been present. This method cannot be used if the pastor has less than two years at the church.

Cost of Living Plus Merit. The minimum annual salary increase should be a cost-of-living raise, along with some sort of merit increase. In the case of a pastor or employee who has demonstrated poor work performance, he or she would not receive a merit increase. Determinations for merit increases could be set by some type of formula established by the personnel committee and approved by the church.

NOTES

1. Bramer, *Efficient Church Business Management*, pp. 115–16.

2. Manfred Holck Jr., *Church Finance in a Complex Economy*, Creative Leadership Series, ed. Lyle E. Schaller (Nashville: Abingdon Press, 1983), p. 101.

3. Pollock, *Business Management*, p. 161.

4. C. Eric Lincoln and Lawrence H. Mamiya, *The Black Church in The African American Experience* (Durham, N.C.: Duke University Press, 1994), p. 126–28. This is the paperback edition. The study looked at the seven major black denominations. As Lincoln and Mamiya pointed out in their study, many of the black Baptist respondents had denominational affiliations with white Baptist denominations, either with Southern Baptists or American Baptists.

5. Fee, "The First Epistle to the Corinthians," p. 392.

6. D. Edmond Hiebert, "First Timothy," *Everyman's Bible Commentary* (Chicago: Moody Press, 1957), p.101.

7. Strauch, *Biblical Eldership*, p. 240.

8. Warren W. Weirsbe, *Be Faithful: 1 & 2 Timothy & Titus* (Wheaton, Ill.: Victor Books, 1981), p. 76.

9. Bramer, op. cit., p. 118.

10. I strongly recommend that those who are responsible for reviewing and recommending salary and benefit packages for the pastor and church staff see Daniel D. Busby, CPA, *The Zondervan Minister's Tax and Financial Guide*, 1996 Edition (Grand Rapids, Mich.: Zondervan Publishing, 1995). Also, by Busby, *The Zondervan Church and Nonprofit Organization Tax and Financial Guide*, 1996 Edition. Also, B. J. Worth, *Income Tax Guide for Ministers and Religious Workers* (Winona Lake, Ind.: World Publishing, 1995).

11. Busby, *Minister's Tax Guide*, 1996 Edition, p. 170.

Chapter Seven

Church Construction: A Pastor's Dream or Nightmare

"Then Solomon said . . . 'I have built thee a lofty house. . . .'"

—*2 Chronicles 6:1–2*

In December 1984, at our annual church meeting, I presented a proposal to the congregation that we undertake a study to determine whether or not we should expand our church facilities. The idea was received with unanimous consent. A study committee was appointed and instructions were issued regarding how they were to go about their work. It seemed to me that this would be a relatively simple process, since everyone at the church meeting thought it was a good idea. You appoint a building committee, they conduct a study to determine how much new space the church will need, you hire an architect, borrow from the bank what you do not raise, build the new building and praise God happily ever after. Well, it's not quite that simple.

I thought like most pastors who have never led a church to build anything. I felt this could not possibly be a difficult process. After all, the Lord was blessing the church. We were growing by leaps and bounds.

The sanctuary, which seated about 275 people, was packed every Sunday. We added an 8:00 A.M. worship service and soon that was starting to fill up. All of the signs were present. We needed a new building. Our existing building had been constructed in 1954 using 1940s architectural designs. At the time it was built, the church did not have a lot of money so the building lacked a lot of modern conveniences. I knew it was time to build!

To make a long story short, an eight year struggle ensued, filled with all kinds of problems and conflicts. Some of the most bitter days of my tenure as pastor revolved around this church construction project. We literally disagreed about everything. We could not agree on such things as the process to select an architect, who should be our attorney, the signing of contracts for services, color schemes, carpet and locations, and who would be in charge of the project. There were no easy decisions for our church.

Construction projects often plunge churches into bitter struggles and conflicts that can have lasting effects on some people. There are personal feelings attached to church construction projects. Members have a personal stake in the outcome of the project. Long time stakeholders are either very supportive or very much against any new construction taking place. In our project I had both.

The dream turned into a nightmare when I discovered that the first architect we hired was not licensed. He had drawn a beautiful drawing of a proposed new building, for a fee of $3,500. It was worthless. He was someone that one of the leaders of the church knew. A great piece of art, but that was all. We had spent the church's money and had nothing to show for it but a picture. From that point on the whole effort was one uphill struggle after another. These kinds of mistakes can plunge the pastor into a real credibility battle. Make sure that you do your homework regarding anyone that you are going to hire at the church's expense.

GET READY FOR STRUGGLE

If you are planning to build a new building, make sure the Lord has sanctioned your effort (see Eccl. 3:1ff.). There is nothing more demanding of a pastor, stressful for the church, and more divisive of a congregation than a building program. It pulls a congregation in many different directions. It leaves the pastor wondering if he did the right thing even suggesting that a new building be built.

There are several key areas of struggle and conflict associated with church construction. First, raising the money to get started. This process can take several years, which wears on the patience of church members who want to see something happening right away. Second, leaders can become a lightening rod of conflict. Some will be very supportive, others will seek to disrupt and destroy the vision. Third, city zoning laws and codes can be a source of great frustration. One of our biggest headaches was meeting the city's parking requirements. When we started, the code required one space per five seats. Halfway through, the code changed from five per seat to three per seat. City building codes can change while you are in the process of planning and alter your project several times. Fourth, you must decide who is going to control the process. Many times the pastor will see this as "his baby" and therefore feel that he should be in complete control. This can drive a wedge between the pastor and the leaders. It's best to get as many of your key leaders on board and tuned into the vision as possible. Their help will be greatly needed. Fifth, the sheer cost of getting a building project into motion is a major obstacle. Many times members may not understand that it costs tremendous amounts of money just to conduct sound building studies. Cost can increase when planners have to be hired to conduct feasibility studies on certain tracts of land. Engineering costs can add up when old buildings are being renovated and no one knows where the original drawings are located. Everything costs and everyone has their hand out. They are all too eager to take the church's money.

PASTORS PAY A PERSONAL TOLL

One of the biggest problems with church construction projects is the emotional and physical toll it takes on the pastor and those closest to him—his family. Everything that could have gone wrong with our project did. It got to a point that I dreaded church business meetings. A few days before each meeting, I would start to develop severe headaches, my stomach would tie itself up in knots, and I could not sleep at night. I never knew what would come up at the meeting, outside of my agenda. Any discussion of the building project would end up in confusion.

All of the meetings of our key leaders revolved around the money that we were spending on the building. There was a feeling that we needed to cut back on our ministries, educational programs, and missions until we finished building. The sentiment was that everything we raised needed to go towards the building program. I resisted that idea.

Because of all of the problems we were having, internally and externally, I started to feel betrayed by some of the church's leaders. My confidence in some of them started to sink to new lows. Any public statements I made about the project had to be guarded, lest they be taken out of context. However, the Lord gave me several key supporters. The chairman of our trustee board and a few others were solidly behind the effort and helped tremendously.

After four years I was a physical and emotional wreck. My family doctor told me that I was developing an ulcer and high blood pressure. My hair had started to turn gray. My face was becoming drawn. I felt paranoid and unloved by members of the church. I started to withdraw from members of my family and the church. The joy of being there was gone and I wanted to leave. At that point I would have gone anywhere to get away. It was a terrible time in my life. I could not understand how something this wonderful could be so difficult.

The problems and delays we experienced had a corresponding negative impact on financial giving to the project. Building fund pledges and contributions to the project slowed to a trickle. Sometimes we would not receive $50 in a week for the project. All the while the costs of building were rising with each new day. One morning while having my private devotional time, I turned to Ecclesiastes 3. I stopped at the third verse that reads, "A time to kill, and a time to heal; a time to tear down, and a time to build up." The Lord told me through His Word that it was not time for us to build. I called a special meeting of the key leaders of the church.

At our meeting, I opened with a hymn, prayer and Scripture. I told them how destructive and divisive the building project had become to our fellowship. I then read Ecclesiastes 3:3 and said, "It's not time for us to build." I announced the adjournment of the meeting and we closed with prayer. For the first time during this entire process I felt relieved. I did not have to explain any more delays nor beg for more money to get the project done.

TAKE YOUR TIME

For nearly two years I did not say much about the project. There was nothing to say. However, all the while we continued to work on all of the preliminary things that needed to be done. I shared my feelings and our progress with the group that met on Tuesday for noonday Bible study and prayer. There were things like zoning requirements, parking, setback requirements, use permits, conditional use permits, utilities hookups, lending requirements, asbestos reports, hazardous waste and environmental impact studies, property purchases, and on and on the challenges went.

Everything associated with a church building project or renovation takes a great deal of time. (The average pastor has no experience in major capital construction campaigns and feels that because Moses built a tabernacle, he or she can build a church building.) I believe that if you stay with your vision, you can build the building you are dreaming of.

Finally, we had crossed every hurdle. We began the process and proceeded to complete the building. The construction phase was one of the most enjoyable times for me. All of the headaches and heartaches were behind. I had matured in many ways. Finally, on Easter Sunday, we marched into our new sanctuary. Everyone was very happy. You would think that that would be the end of a happy story. Unfortunately, it was only the beginning of another long night of pain—paying the monthly mortgage.

I don't want you to think that we had a lot of problems because we were not organized. Our building effort was extremely organized. There were subcommittees for everything. The human element and the stake that people have in the past and the confidence that they put in your ability are major hurdles to overcome in any building effort.

THE PITFALLS OF CHURCH CONSTRUCTION

Building a new church facility is only one side of a multi-dimensional project. Often the headaches can start just after you move into a new building. Suddenly, you are faced with having to make serious decisions and choices about ministry and missions. Let me share some of my experiences and how they may impact upon the cash flow of your church immediately upon finishing a beautiful building.

Pitfall One: Decreased Financial Support and Giving

One of the first experiences will be a decrease in the amount of money given to the church during the first year after completing the project. Much of the increase in giving is money that is directed to the building project. When it's finished, members no longer feel the sense of urgency. Therefore, they cut back on giving.

Make stewardship the heart of your capital fundraising campaign. When members learn to love the Lord in their giving, they will continue to give more than enough to meet your new obligations. Teach stewardship boldly and with much confidence.

Pitfall Two: Underestimating the Operating Costs of the New Building

If you double the size of your facility, guess what? The cost of operating is going to more than double. Insurance premiums skyrocket, utility costs jump, cleaning and maintenance costs go up, there are new staff requirements, equipping the building is expensive. All of these are costs that the same folks who were housed in a smaller building must now pay. Jesus said, "For which of you, when he wants to build a tower does not sit down and calculate the cost, to see if he has enough to complete it? Otherwise, when he has laid the foundation, and is not able to finish, all who observe it begin to ridicule him, saying, This man began to build and was not able to finish" (Luke 12:28–30).

Make sure that you conduct a sound financial analysis of the cost associated with operating a larger building. The local power company can give you estimates for heating and cooling the building. Look at yours after construction costs. They will be much greater than your previous cost.

Pitfall Three: The Belief That a New Building Will Spawn Instant, Immediate Growth

New church buildings rarely produce any significant, immediate growth in membership. There will be the customary rush to see the new building and worship in it, but when that thrill is gone so are the church-hoppers. What will make your church grow are the things that made it grow prior to launching the building project. If you cut out your ministry to save money, you in effect take away one of the evangelistic vehicles for drawing new members. Building to draw new members is not a good reason to build.

Pitfall Four: The Belief That If You Build It the People Will Happily Pay For the New Building

Once the reality sets in that your church has a heavy debt load, some of the members will start to complain. Every dollar spent to service debt and pay interest robs the church of resources for ministry. A million dollar debt load, at 9 percent, will cost you in the neighborhood of $80–90,000 a year in interest alone. If your congregation is not willing to prepay the mortgage, it will pay almost double for the building in principle and interest payments. It's better and more cost effective to raise the money in advance for new construction or renovation. Borrowing places a heavy burden on the church. "The rich rules over the poor, And the borrower *becomes* the lender's slave" (Prov. 22:7).

Pitfall Five: Failing to Make a Long-Range Financial Plan

As a leader you must anticipate the worst case. You cannot rely on the weekly tithes and offerings to ensure the long-term financial viability of the church. A portion of each week's offering needs to be set aside and invested for long term growth. The money could be invested in a diversified portfolio of mutual funds or blue-chip stocks or high-yield treasury notes or high-yield corporate bonds.

In Genesis 41 when Joseph interpreted the dream of the Pharaoh of Egypt, he told him that God was showing him that an economic downturn was coming. Joseph told the Pharaoh that he needed to set aside a portion of each harvest for the next seven years and thereby he would avoid catastrophe when the famine came upon the land.

Pitfall Six: Cutting Corners to Save Money

There is the belief that if you always take the lowest bid you will save the church a lot of money. Usually when you cut corners on a building project, it ends up costing you more to fix the corner. Carefully evaluate your project in light of your costs, but don't let costs be the determining factor in your decisions. Remember, nothing is free.

Pitfall Seven: Naive Pastors and Building Committees

Pastors are really out of their league when it comes to church construction projects. Even lay people who may do contract work, or have a small electrical firm or plumbing business, are really out of their league when it comes to major construction projects. The best thing that a pastor can do is to educate himself and his people on what is involved with a construction project. Often we trust architects, who are notorious for making design promises that cannot be fulfilled and will give you cost estimates that are sometimes unrealistic. Do your homework! Churches should only work with licensed architects, contractors, and architectural firms who can be fully bonded and insured for the value of the project. Everything should be in writing, including contracts, job specifications, and correspondence between the church and the architect.

Pitfall Eight: Not Using Your Leaders

Many pastors will make the mistake of not using their leaders to help lead their building projects. I learned one lesson during the process: until the leaders see your vision, it will not materialize without much pain and sorrow. Spend time helping your leaders to understand the vision. Empower the chairman of your trustee board to provide leadership and give him authority to make a lot of major decisions. Establish close ties with your deacons and deaconesses. These are usually going to be some of your biggest and most consistent financial supporters. Their help, prayers, and support will go a long way to speeding up the construction process.

GET PROFESSIONAL FINANCIAL HELP

In any building project you will need a financial team, just like you have a design-build team. Money is the critical element in every building program. It may not be a bad practice to sit down with your banker early on in the process and let him assist you in developing a sound financial plan. He can assist you with developing a three-to-five-year savings and investment strategy that will help your church reach its goal of paying cash for its new church building. If the church cannot fully pay for the new building, by saving and investing wisely, it would at least have a sizeable down payment.

There is a school of thought that believes that the church should not save or set money aside for the future. I believe that kind of thinking reflects poor stewardship. In the future, it will be necessary to develop long range financial plans that have an element of investing as a part of their mix. After all, didn't Jesus tell a parable in Matthew 25:14ff about a man who had three servants to whom he entrusted certain sums of money. Jesus said that two of the servants were rewarded because they invested and doubled their master's money. The third servant took his master's money and buried it in the ground. He took no risks, therefore he had no gain; he lost everything. As a result of his poor stewardship, he was cast into outer darkness.

The kingdom of God will continue to grow. This is a great time to be alive and involved in the work of kingdom building. God has given us an abundance of resources. The question is, are we able to effectively and efficiently manage them to create the greatest value for the kingdom of God. Those of us who are charged with the steward-ship of the church's resources will need to become as wise with God's gifts as the children of this world have with their gifts.

Epilogue

Ten Areas That Impact Money Management

1. Inflation and Deflation
2. Personnel
3. Physical Facilities—Buildings and Grounds
4. Non-Durable Supplies
5. Expanding Ministries and Missions
6. Equipment
7. Federal, State and Local Taxes
8. Safety and Security
9. Maintenance and Repair/Replacement Costs
10. External Social and Economic Changes

Bibliography

Barrett, C. K. "The First Epistle to the Corinthians." *Black's New Testament Commentary.* Peabody, Mass.: Hendrickson Publishers, 1968.

Bloss, Julie L. J. D., CEBS. *Church Law and Tax Report: The Church Guide to Employment Law.* Matthews, N.C.: Christian Ministry Resources, 1993.

Bowman, Ray with Hall, Eddy. *When Not to Build: An Architect's Unconditional Wisdom for the Growing Church.* Foreword by Charles Arn. Grand Rapids, Mich.: Baker Book House, 1992.

Bramer, John C. *Efficient Church Business Management.* Philadelphia: The Westminster Press, 1960.

Busby, Daniel D., CPA. *The Zondervan Minister's Tax and Financial Guide,* 1996 Edition. Grand Rapids, Mich.: Zondervan Publishing House, 1995.

————. *The Zondervan Church and Nonprofit Organization Tax Financial Guide,* 1996 Edition. Grand Rapids, Mich.: Zondervan Publishing House, 1995.

Dale, Robert D. *Pastoral Leadership: A Handbook of Resources for Effective Congregational Leadership.* 5th printing. Nashville: Abingdon, 1991.

————. *To Dream Again: How to Help Your Church Come Alive.* Nashville: Broadman Press, 1981.

Drucker, Peter F. *Managing the Non-Profit Organization: Principles and Practices.* New York: Harper Business, 1990.

Earle, Ralph. "1, 2 Timothy." In Volume 11 of *The Expositors Bible Commentary*, edited by Frank E. Gaebelein. Grand Rapids, Mich.: Zondervan Publishing House, 1978.

Fee, Gordon D. "The First Epistle to the Corinthians." In *The New International Commentary on the New Testament*. Grand Rapids, Mich.: William B. Eerdmans Publishing Company, 1987.

Harris, James H. *Pastoral Theology: A Black Church Perspective*. Minneapolis: Fortress Press, 1991.

Henry, Jack A. *Basic Accounting for Churches: A Turnkey Manual*. Nashville: Broadman & Holman Publishers, 1994.

————. *Basic Budgeting for Churches: A Complete Guide*. Nashville: Broadman & Holman Publishers, 1995.

Hiebert, D. Edmond. "First Timothy." In *Everyman's Bible Commentary*. Chicago: Moody Press, 1957.

Holck, Manfred, Jr. *Church Finance in a Complex Economy. Creative Leadership Series*, edited by Lyle Schaller. Nashville: Abingdon Press, 1983.

House, H. Wayne. *Christian Ministries and the Law*. Grand Rapids, Mich.: Baker Book House, 1992.

Lincoln, C. Eric and Mamiya, Lawrence H. *The Black Church in the African American Experience*. Durham, N.C.: Duke University Press, 1994.

MacArthur, John, Jr. "1 Corinthians," In *The MacArthur New Testament Commentary*. Chicago: Moody Press, 1984.

————. *The Master's Plan for the Church*. Chicago: Moody Press, 1991.

Maxwell, John C. *Developing the Leader Within You*. Nashville: Thomas Nelson, Inc., 1993.

McLeod, Thomas E. *The Work of the Church Treasurer*. Rev. ed. Valley Forge, Pa.: Judson Press, 1992.

Pollock, David R. *Business Management in the Local Church*. Foreword by Larry Burkett. Chicago: Moody Press, 1990.

Powers, Bruce, ed. *Church Administration Handbook*. Nashville: Broadman Press, 1985.

Stott, John R. W. "The Epistles of John." *Tyndale New Testament Commentaries*. Grand Rapids, Mich.: William B. Eerdmans Publishing Company, 1983.

Strauch, Alexander. *Biblical Eldership: An Urgent Call to Restore Biblical Church Leadership*. 2d ed. Littleton, Colo.: Lewis and Roth Publishers, 1988.

Strauch, Alexander. *The New Testament Deacon: Minister of Mercy.* Littleton, Colo.: Lewis and Roth Publishers, 1992.

Tennyson, Mack. *Church Finances for People Who Count: A Basic Handbook for Church Treasurers, Trustees, Deacons, and Ministry Staff.* Grand Rapids, Mich.: Zondervan Publishing, 1990.

Tibbetts, Orlando L. *The Work of the Church Trustee.* Valley Forge, Pa.: Judson Press, 1981.

Vine, W. E. *Vines's Expository Dictionary of New Testament Words.* Peabody, Mass.: Hendrickson Publishers.

White, Robert N. Editor. *Managing Today's Church.* Valley Forge, Pa.: Judson Press, 1981.

Wiersbe, Warren W. *Be Faithful: 1 & 2 Timothy and Titus.* 7th printing. Wheaton, Ill.: Victor Books, 1986.

Worth, B. J. *Income Tax Guide for Ministers and Religious Workers.* Winona Lake, Ind.: World Publishing, 1995.